## ROBERT HOLMAN

Robert Holman was born in 1952 and brought up on a farm
in North Yorkshire. He was awarded an Arts Council Writers'
Bursary in 1974, and since then he has spent periods as
resident dramatist with the Royal National Theatre and with
the Royal Shakespeare Company in Stratford-upon-Avon.
He has written extensively for both theatre and television, and
his stage plays, including *Outside the Whale*, *German Skerries*,
for which he won the George Devine Award, *Other Worlds*,
*Today*, *Making Noise Quietly*, *Across Oka*, *Rafts and Dreams*
and *Bad Weather* have been seen in cities as far apart as Los
Angeles and Tokyo, following their premieres at such theatres
as the Royal Court, the RSC, the Bush and the Edinburgh
Traverse. His first novel, *The Amish Landscape*, was published
in 1992.

Robert Holman

# HOLES
# IN THE SKIN

NICK HERN BOOKS
London
www.nickhernbooks.co.uk

**A Nick Hern Book**

*Holes in the Skin* first published in 2003 as a paperback original
by Nick Hern Books, 14 Larden Road, London W3 7ST.

*Holes in the the Skin* copyright © 2003 by Robert Holman

Robert Holman has asserted his right to be identified
as the author of this work

Front cover photo: Clare Park

Typeset by Country Setting, Kingsdown, Kent, CT14 8ES
Printed in Great Britain by CLE Press, St Ives, Cambs PE27 3LE

ISBN 1 8545 747 7

A CIP catalogue record for this book is available
from the British Library

TO PIPPA

## Chichester Festival Theatre

*This new theatre, affording new shape (for the last 400 years at least), new ideas, new functions, new thinking.*

Laurence Olivier

Chichester Festival Theatre was built in 1962. Funded by public subscription, it was the brainchild of a local optician and councillor, Leslie Evershed-Martin who also persuaded Laurence Olivier to become the first Artistic Director. It was here that Olivier nurtured the ideas and actors that were to shape the first National Theatre seasons, and Chichester remained a summer home for the National Theatre company until 1965. The Festival Theatre's hexagonal thrust stage saw the first performances of such productions as Olivier's *Othello,* Olivier and Michael Redgrave in *Uncle Vanya*, Joan Plowright in *St Joan*, premieres of plays by Peter Shaffer and John Arden, performed by an ensemble which included Maggie Smith, Derek Jacobi, Michael Gambon and Robert Stephens.

In subsequent years Chichester became associated with productions of classic plays featuring internationally renowned actors. Lauren Bacall, Alan Bates, Ingrid Bergman, Kenneth Branagh, Judi Dench, John Gielgud, Alec Guinness, Omar Sharif, Topol, Kathleen Turner and Peter Ustinov are amongst the actors who have appeared in works by Shakespeare, Shaw, Ibsen, Brecht, Chekhov and Wilde.

The opening of the Minerva Studio Theatre in 1989 (whose first Artistic Director was Sam Mendes) enabled Chichester to explore the work of contemporary British writers such as Caryl Churchill, Terry Johnson and Peter Whelan. In recent years the Minerva has shown work exclusively by living writers and in 2003 all four productions are premieres. The Minerva has also provided a home for an extensive programme of community and education work. Today the Chichester Festival Youth Theatre is one of the largest in the region.

2003 marks the beginning of a new era in the history of Chichester Festival Theatre. The new Artistic Directors, Martin Duncan, Ruth Mackenzie and Steven Pimlott, have returned to many of Olivier's original ideas. An ensemble of actors and musicians who work together throughout the summer is once again at the heart of the festival. In both theatres a single flexible 'installation' provides the backdrop for all the productions. In addition a theme has been chosen to provide a focus for the wide array of activities taking place during the Festival. For 2003 the theme is Venice, leading to productions of Gilbert and Sullivan's *The Gondoliers* and Shakespeare's *The Merchant of Venice* in the Festival Theatre, Fassbinder's version of Goldoni's *The Coffee House* and a new work by the Brothers Marquez, *I Caught My Death in Venice*, in the Minerva, with an epic youth theatre performance of *Pinocchio* taking place in the park outside the theatre. Other productions take themes that ripple outwards from this Venetian starting point. Water lies at the heart both of a new adaptation of Charles Kingsley's *The Water Babies* and Chekhov's *The Seagull*, while *Nathan the Wise* mirrors the religious conflict of *The Merchant of Venice* and Robert Holman's new play *Holes in the Skin* provides a striking companion piece to *The Water Babies*. The festival themes are further explored and developed through talks, rehearsed readings, concerts and promenades.

*For further information about the 2003 and future Chichester Festival Theatre seasons visit* www.cft.org.uk.

## The 2003 Ensemble

Daniel Abelson
Marion Bailey
Natasha Bain
Julie Barnes
Desmond Barrit
Steven Beard
Alfred Burke
Sarah Cattle
Trevor Conner
Deborah Crowe
Jonathan Cullen
Kay Curram
Niamh Cusack
Alicia Davies
Owen Dennis
Noma Dumezweni
Fiona Dunn
Steve Elias
Kevin Elliot
Steven Fawell
Ricky Fearon
Michael Feast
Sheila Gish
Louise Gold
Jane Hazelgrove
Benjamin Hess
Kieran Hill
David Hounslow
Darlene Johnson
Jeffery Kissoon
Mark Lacey
Paul Leonard
Simon Lys
John Marquez
Martin Marquez
Barry McCarthy
Neil McDermott
Joe McGann
Dido Miles
Alex Moen
Jo Nesbitt
Sasha Oakley
Katherine O'Shea

Jamie Parker
Christian Patterson
Megan Pound
Liza Pulman
Philip Quast
Benedict Quirke
Patrick Robinson
James Saxon
Andrew Sheridan
Joe Shovelton
Nicola Sloane
Peter Sproule
Ed Stoppard
Geoffrey Streatfeild
Robert Swann
Fraser Tannock
Mark Taylor
Timothy Taylorson
Adam Tedder
Stephen Ventura
Julie Webb
Jenni Workman
Robert Workman

*Associate Sound Designer*
Paul Arditti

*Associate Composer*
Jason Carr

*Associate Designer*
(*Festival Theatre*)
Alison Chitty

*Associate Dramaturg*
Edward Kemp

*Associate Choreographer*
Jonathan Lunn

*Associate Designer*
(*Minerva Theatre*)
Ashley Martin-Davies

*Associate Artist*
Joe McGann

*Associate Lighting Designer*
Peter Mumford

*Holes in the Skin* was first performed at the Chichester Festival Theatre on 13 June 2003, with the following cast:

| | |
|---|---|
| KERRY | Sarah Cattle |
| DENNIS | David Hounslow |
| HAZEL COOPER | Jane Hazelgrove |
| LEE | Andrew Sheridan |
| EWAN PEACOCK | Daniel Abelson |
| FREYA | Marion Bailey |
| DOMINIC | Jamie Parker |
| JOACHIM SOERENSEN | Peter Sproule |

*Director* Simon Usher
*Designer* Anthony Lamble
*Lighting Designer* Simon Bennison
*Sound Designer* Angela McCluney
*Composer* Neil McArthur
*Assistant Director* Martin Constantine
*Costume Supervisor* Laura Hunt
*Company Stage Manager* Amelia Ferrand-Rook
*Stage Manager* Suzanne Bourke
*Deputy Stage Manager* Kathryn Croft
*Assistant Stage Manager* Charlotte A. Harley

**Characters**

KERRY

DENNIS

HAZEL COOPER

LEE

EWAN PEACOCK

FREYA

DOMINIC

JOACHIM SOERENSEN

Voices of Sheryl, Dean and Policeman

**Act One**

**Act Two**

*The play takes place in the present day.*

## ACT ONE

### Scene One

*The living room of a council house in Stokesley. A morning in July.*

*There is a sofa and a glass-topped dining-table. On the floor, near to two dirty plates, is a sauce bottle and a glass ashtray full of cigarette ends. There are some empty lager cans and two glass tumblers. On the table is a bottle of vodka, salt, the wrapping off the chips, and a tray. Sunlight is flooding in through a gap in the curtains.*

KERRY *enters with a mug of tea, eating toast, listening to a Walkman. She is fifteen years old, has a white face and her hair is tied back with coloured bands. She is wearing school uniform, though it is incomplete. She puts the mug on the table, steps over the mess, draws the curtains and opens the window. She does not hear the voices that come in from outside, and sets about tidying up the room, emptying the ashtray onto the chip paper and picking up the plates. She puts the toast between her teeth.*

*Sheryl.* You're a policeman, you sort it out. Ask him why he shouts no matter what.

*Policeman.* She wants to know why you're always shouting.

*Dean.* Ask her why she burns me boiled egg no matter what day it is.

*Sheryl.* Yer can't burn boiled eggs.

*Dean.* I'm talking about me bloody toast.

*Policeman.* Dean, calm down.

*Dean.* Ask her why she never bloody does me egg for three and a half minutes.

*Sheryl.* Ask him why he chucked the timer at the floor more like.

*Dean.* Tell her I was chucking it at her.

*Policeman.* Are you going to let him back in or not?

*Sheryl.* No.

*Dean.* Tell her I'll smash another of her windows. Tell her I couldn't give a toss about her or her lousy kid.

*Sheryl.* Ask him why he moved in when no one wanted him to.

*Dean.* Ask her how I've fuckin' treated her. Go on. She doesn't know what luxury is.

*Policeman.* Dean, listen to me, calm down.

*Dean.* All I ask is for a fuckin' egg done for fuckin' three and a half minutes and fuckin' toast that don't look like it's been in a fuckin' fire.

KERRY *scrunches up the chip paper. She picks up the empty cans and tumblers and puts them on the table.*

*Next door, glass smashes as a window breaks.*

*Policeman.* That was a very stupid thing to do.

*Sheryl.* Ask him why he acts like a short-trousered wanker.

*Dean.* Ask her what it means, if she knows.

*Sheryl.* Yer act like a big kid.

*Dean.* Yer hardly pretty, Sheryl.

*Sheryl.* Am I pretty?

*Policeman.* It's not up to me to say.

*Dean.* Yer've got some bottle, I'll give yer that, yer twat. Yer the first copper who's dared show his face round here all year.

KERRY *goes to the sofa. She tidies up some teenage magazines.*

*Policeman.* Are you going to let him back in or not, Sheryl?

*Sheryl.* Ask him if he's going to mend the windows?

*Policeman.* Are you?

*Dean.* Tell her I'll fuckin' die first.

*Policeman.* There's your answer.

*Dean.* Ask her why she's ugly as shit.

*Sheryl.* Ask him why he was saying the opposite last night.

*Policeman.* Dean, you'd better just leave.

*Dean.* You know you fuckin' love us, Sheryl.

*Sheryl.* I wouldn't love you if you was the last person on earth.

> KERRY *is plumping up the cushions on the sofa. She has not seen* DENNIS.

> DENNIS *has come in. He is thirty eight years old, thin as a rake with greasy black hair. He is wearing a white vest and pants. He has seen* KERRY *and stopped.*

DENNIS. Are you yer mam's kid?

*Policeman.* She's made her point of view very clear, she wants you to go.

*Sheryl.* I don't. I want him to act proper for once in his baby life.

*Dean.* Ask her why she's lovey one minute and fuckin' useless the next.

*Sheryl.* Ask him why he can't control his temper.

*Dean.* Ask her why she dialled 999 when there's no need.

*Policeman.* You were breaking down the door.

*Dean.* It's my poxy door. I can fuckin' break it if I want to, can't I?

DENNIS. Cloth ears.

*Sheryl.* Ask him if he's going to act responsible from now on?

*Policeman.* Are you, Dean?

*Dean.* Ask her if she'll do me an egg, proper like.

*Policeman.* Will you do him an egg?

*Sheryl.* I might.

*Dean.* Ask her if the yolk'll be nice and runny for me soldiers.

*Policeman.* I know how difficult it is to judge a boiled egg.

*Dean.* Who asked you owt? Yer not wanted round here. Fuck off where you belong.

> KERRY *has become aware that someone is there. She takes off the headphones and turns.*

KERRY. Who are you when you're at home?

DENNIS. I asked you if you was yer mam's lass about ten minutes ago.

KERRY. Who else would I be?

KERRY *continues to tidy up. She puts everything onto the tray on the table.*

*Policeman.* Dean, I can arrest you for disorderly conduct.

*Dean.* Ask him why he's fucking arresting me all of a sudden when I've done nowt, why don't yer.

*Sheryl.* Yeh, why are you arresting him?

*Policeman.* I'm not arresting him, I said I could arrest him.

*Sheryl.* Yer neither use nor ornament. Yer still in nappies.

*Dean.* You tell him, Sheryl.

*Sheryl.* Yer somebody's son, I suppose somebody buys you a birthday present. It's my birthday. Not that he's bloody bothered. He's right as usual, yer not wanted round here. I'm surprised you've got the bloody nerve.

DENNIS *has gone to the window. He peers out.*

DENNIS. Fucking police.

DENNIS *shuts the window.*

KERRY *sits at the table to eat what is left of her toast. The sunlight catches her face.*

HAZEL COOPER *comes in. She is thirty four years old, small and wiry with strong, angular features. She is wearing a negligee.*

HAZEL. Have you found it or what?

DENNIS. I've looked everywhere, petal.

HAZEL *begins to search the room.* DENNIS *looks at* KERRY.

What's she called?

HAZEL. Call her what you like.

DENNIS. What's yer name?

KERRY. What's it to you?

DENNIS. I won't ask you again.

KERRY. Good.

DENNIS. You were lucky I asked once.

HAZEL *looks under the cushions on the sofa.*

KERRY. Yer made a mess.

HAZEL. Yer cleaned it up, what yer on about.

KERRY. Yer made a mess again, I meant.

HAZEL *looks at her daughter.*

HAZEL. Have you seen it?

KERRY. Seen what?

HAZEL. If I was you I'd be a lot more carefuller.

KERRY. I don't know what yer on at.

HAZEL. My video. Have you taken it?

KERRY. What would I want it for?

HAZEL. How would I know. You tell me. You'd pinch owt as long as it wasn't yours.

KERRY. Which video?

HAZEL. I've already warned you to be a lot more carefuller. I don't say things twice.

KERRY. Yer just have.

HAZEL. My sexy video. The one you've hidden.

KERRY. Were you going to watch it with him, as if I didn't know.

HAZEL. His name's Dennis.

DENNIS *nods at* KERRY.

DENNIS. Now then.

HAZEL. Dennis is staying with us for a bit, until he can sort himself out.

KERRY. Looks like he'll be here for ages then.

DENNIS. It's a good job I like lasses like you, pet.

KERRY. I'm not bothered about being liked.

DENNIS. Yeh, I can tell.

HAZEL *looks at* KERRY.

HAZEL. Where is it?

KERRY. How would I know?

HAZEL. She takes them to school and sells them. It's a little income she's got going.

KERRY. I wouldn't touch them if you paid me. Great butch men humping each other. It's disgusting. It's not even funny. You won't be here long, yer not even slightly butch.

DENNIS. She knows how to be cheeky does your lass.

KERRY. I must have caught it off you.

HAZEL *sits on the sofa.*

HAZEL. Yer make clutter like other people make space.

KERRY. What's that mean?

HAZEL. It means yer always around.

KERRY. I live here.

HAZEL. That's my worst luck.

KERRY. Yeh, it is.

KERRY *drinks tea.*

DENNIS *sits on the sofa. He puts his arm around* HAZEL.

DENNIS. It's a well-known fact that teenagers are mixed up. If yer needed proof it's in her.

KERRY. She gets all randy over videos meant for gays.

DENNIS. Has she made you sulky, pet?

HAZEL. She hasn't made me anything.

DENNIS. You've gone and put yer mam in a bad mood.

KERRY. Who has?

DENNIS *tickles* HAZEL.

DENNIS. That lass of yours, there's no stopping her once she gets going.

HAZEL *sticks out her tongue.*

HAZEL. There's no stopping you, Dennis. Yer a menace.

DENNIS *blows and whispers in her ear. The tickling makes* HAZEL *giggle.*

DENNIS. I'll tell yer, petal. She's nothing but trouble.

HAZEL. She's only trouble if yer let her be.

HAZEL *giggles.* DENNIS *nibbles at her ear, almost swallows it.*

DENNIS. You don't let her be, I suppose.

HAZEL. She knows where she is with me.

DENNIS. She's all over you. She needs more than a bit of discipline that one.

HAZEL. Are you going to give it to her, Dennis?

DENNIS. She needs her panties taken down and her bottom given a good smack.

HAZEL *sticks out her tongue.*

HAZEL. She won't thank yer for it.

DENNIS. She will in the long run.

KERRY. Yer about as funny as being dead, which is what you are.

DENNIS *tickles her.* HAZEL *giggles.*

HAZEL. We're only joking, Kerry. Yer can take a bit of fun on a bright Tuesday morning, can't yer? Stop making the world miserable and give us a smile for once. Get off me. Tell him to get off us, Kerry. Tell him he's got hands worse than an octopus.

KERRY. It's not as if he didn't hear yer, mam.

DENNIS. She's sulking now. You're a right pair of sulks.

HAZEL. Tell him to take a running jump for us, Kerry.

DENNIS. You know you like me fingers going where fingers go.

HAZEL *stands up.*

What's up with yer?

HAZEL. What's up with you.

DENNIS. What's up with you all of a sudden?

HAZEL *adjusts her negligee.*

I was right the first time.

HAZEL. What were you ever right about?

DENNIS. Yer moods, that's what I'm right about.

HAZEL. Bully for you.

DENNIS. Yeh, bully for me. Yer dozy bloody sod.

KERRY *drinks tea.*

I know why she's like she is.

*He looks at* HAZEL.

You need help from someone, pet. It'll be too late sooner than yer realise.

HAZEL. Ask him who he thinks he is.

KERRY. She wants to know who you think you are.

DENNIS. Ask her why she's full of moods.

KERRY. Ask her yourself.

*A slight pause.*

I said you wouldn't be here long.

DENNIS. Shut your face.

HAZEL. Ask him if he wants some toast or something.

KERRY. Do you want some toast or something?

DENNIS. Yeh.

HAZEL *kisses him on the forehead.*

HAZEL. Just another joke, Dennis.

HAZEL *goes out.*

KERRY *drinks tea.*

DENNIS. She's a mind of her own, I'll give yer that.

KERRY. I don't know why you're so clever when you don't look it.

DENNIS. Am I? The world's full of idiots. It's not hard.

*He gets to his feet.*

She was randy as a cockerel a while back.

KERRY *puts her mug on the tray. She stands up and takes a plastic carrier bag off one of the dining chairs. In it are her things for school. She looks through them.*

You remind me of my boy, little Dennis. He can be awkward as hell and no use. He drives yer to distraction.

KERRY *looks through the coloured pens in her pencil case.*

Yer not saying much.

KERRY. I've nothing to say, especially to you.

*A slight pause.*

DENNIS. Will yer mam be making us some tea?

KERRY. Go and ask her.

KERRY *looks through a ring-bound file.*

DENNIS. Little Dennis is so slack about homework he don't do any, not that I've seen.

KERRY. I've got exams.

DENNIS. This morning, pet?

KERRY. Yeh, and this aft'.

DENNIS. You leave early, don't yer.

KERRY. I've got to get the bus to Dormanstown. It takes ages.

DENNIS. Is that where yer go?

KERRY. Why don't yer ask us another obvious question.

DENNIS *pauses.*

DENNIS. Yer all right. Yer a good kid.

*He goes to KERRY at the table.*

What yer looking at?

KERRY. All the science stuff I've got. I've heaps of it.

DENNIS. Yer an extremely tidy writer.

*He puts his arm around her shoulder.*

Yer should see what little Dennis does, pet. I'll have to get him over so he can see how it's done.

*His hand goes down* KERRY*'s spine to her bottom. She stiffens slightly.*

Yer don't want to take any notice of yer mam. There's no being polite to her.

*He squeezes her bottom.* KERRY *moves away.*

What's the matter with yer?

KERRY. What's the matter with you, more like.

DENNIS. Being friendly. What's up? Yer odd or something?

KERRY. You're the one who's odd.

DENNIS. If yer can't have a laugh, what can yer have? Yer need to look t'yer laurels, pet.

KERRY. I wouldn't have you touch us if you was twenty years younger and won the lottery.

DENNIS. I've won the lottery, so there.

*He grabs her hand.*

Come on, Kerry. You know yer ready for it.

*She tries to free her hand, but* DENNIS *is stronger than he looks.*

KERRY. Get off us.

DENNIS. Yer'll be all right with me. I can learn yer.

KERRY. Leave us alone.

DENNIS *puts his arm around her waist and pulls her close.*

DENNIS. What's the matter with yer?

*He tries to kiss her.*

KERRY. Please. Please don't.

*He kisses her on the lips.* KERRY *becomes almost still.*

DENNIS. That was good. That's better, isn't it. Yer much nicer when yer not bolshy.

KERRY. I've got to go.

DENNIS. I've not learnt yer nothing yet.

KERRY. I'm going to miss the bus.

DENNIS *puts his hand up inside her skirt.*

DENNIS. I'll take yer later on. What yer worried about?

KERRY. I don't want yer to.

DENNIS. Have yer got little white knickers on? Yer have. I can feel them. What d'you do with those little white knickers when yer take them off? I bet you enjoy it, don't yer.

KERRY *shakes her head slightly.*

KERRY. No.

DENNIS. You know you do.

KERRY. Please. I'll give you anything you want.

DENNIS. You've only one thing to give me, Kerry.

*He kisses her. He lifts his head.*

Don't be frightened of us. I love you.

HAZEL *comes in.*

HAZEL. What d'you want on your toast, Dennis? Jam or Marmite?

DENNIS *has let* KERRY *go.*

DENNIS. The little sod was being so rude, it's time she was taught a lesson. I tried being polite to her. No response at all.

HAZEL. She's always rude. There's nowt no one can do about it.

DENNIS. I'll have Marmite please.

HAZEL. Save yer energy and give up before you start.

DENNIS. I tried being ultra-nice. I got a response that yer couldn't even warm up. What is it with your lass?

HAZEL. She's twisted in the head.

DENNIS. I asked her all about herself. I asked her about school. No response to either. I told her all about little Dennis. You could put what I got back on a postage stamp. I'll leave you to deal with her tantrums from now on. I'm bloody sick of her. Life's too short for her problems.

DENNIS *sits on the sofa.*

HAZEL. See who you've gone and upset? It's always the same when I bring someone back. I have a life. It's my life. If you're going to stay here, you keep off it.

DENNIS. I offered to do her homework for her. No bloody response that I heard. She's hidden that video of yours. She told us.

HAZEL. Have yer? Yer little sod.

DENNIS. She needs sorting out before she does some damage.

HAZEL. She's not bad sometimes.

DENNIS. She's not bad when yer don't see her.

HAZEL. She's my flesh and blood, Dennis.

DENNIS. You should get rid of her. I don't like it when I see trouble. I can't live with a lot of disagreements.

HAZEL *looks* DENNIS *in the eye and leaves a short silence.*

HAZEL. I might not trust you. I haven't decided.

DENNIS. Don't you have any marmalade, pet?

HAZEL. Don't like it, don't eat it.

DENNIS. Get us some in. I like a spot of marmalade of a morning.

HAZEL. Where's the money coming from till Friday?

DENNIS. Fish some out me trousers. There's some pound coins.

HAZEL. I'm going to look. There'd better be.

HAZEL *goes out.*

*Silence for a moment.*

DENNIS. If I was you, I'd get used to the idea that I was here.

KERRY *goes to the file. She turns over the pages.*

You could be pretty if yer did something with yourself. I'll help yer.

*A slight pause.*

I can't stand silence though. I can't stand moody sods.

DENNIS *gets up.*

Yer want to relax a bit, take it easy with yourself.

KERRY. I couldn't care less.

DENNIS. Couldn't care was made to care. I am moving in yer know.

KERRY. Who says?

DENNIS. I do. Yer mam says.

KERRY. Me mam'll say owt.

DENNIS. You've nice-looking tits.

KERRY. You'll say owt an' all.

DENNIS. I'm only commenting.

KERRY. Keep your comments to yourself.

DENNIS. Yer might at least try to like us. I'm not bad when you get to know me.

*KERRY puts the file and the pencil case in the carrier bag.*

Say you'll try.

KERRY. Try what?

DENNIS. Liking us. I mean, I'm prepared to help you in all sorts of ways. It's the best offer yer'll get. I mean it, Kerry. I like yer mam. Me and her could have a good thing going if you don't wreck it.

*KERRY picks up the carrier bag and the tray. She goes out as HAZEL comes in with a plate of toast and two mugs of tea.*

HAZEL. What's up with her suddenly? I wish she'd warn us when she's got a bonk on.

*She puts the plate and the mugs on the floor near the sofa, and sits down. DENNIS picks up a piece of toast.*

DENNIS. Don't you believe in butter?

HAZEL. There's some on, what yer on about. It's Tuesday.

*HAZEL eats some toast. DENNIS sits beside her.*

If yer don't like it yer know what yer can do.

DENNIS. Only pointing it out.

HAZEL. She must have used it all.

DENNIS. I get better than this at home.

HAZEL. Go and get it then.

> DENNIS *picks up a mug of tea.* HAZEL *shows him the pound coins that have been hidden in her palm.*

I took two to be going on with.

DENNIS. What d'yer know, yer a thief an' all.

HAZEL. I don't know nothing.

DENNIS. Most of us know something, petal.

> HAZEL *sticks out her tongue, sexily.*

HAZEL. I don't. I wish I did.

DENNIS. It's impossible to know nothing.

## Scene Two

*The playground. Early evening of the same day.*

*There are some swings and a seesaw in front of a red brick wall that is covered in graffiti. Some of the messages have been painted over or scrubbed out, but 'Stokesley Boys 97', in yellow paint, is still prominent.*

*The heat of the evening is creating a mirage on the asphalt below the swings.* KERRY *is sitting on one of them. She is bathed in sunlight. The carrier bag is not far away.*

LEE *comes on. He is eighteen years old. He is quite thin with short, light coloured hair, and he has an ear stud. He is wearing jeans and a sweatshirt.*

KERRY *sort of takes an interest in him and ignores him at the same time.*

KERRY. Something wrong?

LEE. You tell us.

> KERRY *starts to swing.*

KERRY. If you're after something why don't you spit it out.

> LEE *puts his foot through the handle in the carrier bag and lifts it up. He takes hold of it and puts it on the swing beside her.*

LEE. You make enemies a lot quicker than yer make friends.

KERRY. I do where you're concerned.

LEE *pauses.*

LEE. Have you come to live in Stokesley?

KERRY. What's it to you?

LEE. Have you come to live with yer mam?

KERRY. Same answer.

LEE. I don't know what to call you.

KERRY. Yer still don't. Call us what you want, see if I care.

LEE *catches the swing so that* KERRY *is left hanging at an angle.*

LEE. You don't seem to be bothered about making friends.

KERRY. You must be clever because you're always spot on.

LEE *pushes her.* KERRY *swings higher.*

LEE. I'm about the best there is round here.

KERRY. I'll go without then, big head.

LEE *pushes her.*

LEE. Is yer mam out?

KERRY. She might be, she might not be.

LEE. Have you lost your key?

KERRY. I might have, I might not have.

KERRY *jumps off the swing. She sits on the seesaw.*

LEE. Have you got a fag on yer?

KERRY. If I had I wouldn't give it to you.

LEE. You do smoke. I've seen you like a chimney.

KERRY. Is it a crime?

LEE. I never said it was.

LEE *sits on the other end of the seesaw. They go up and down.*

Have you a quid you could borrow us?

KERRY. If I had a pound to lend I'd be spending it on meself.

*LEE stands with the seesaw between his legs so that it stops moving.*

LEE. You could answer something I've asked yer.

KERRY. Like what?

LEE. I've given you a big enough list.

KERRY. Me mam's out. I haven't got a key.

*They go up and down.*

LEE. You've been here a week and you haven't got a key. It's a bit mean of her, isn't it?

KERRY. It's not my fault I've been here a week. I didn't want to come here in the first place. It's a dump.

LEE. You'll get to like it, maybe.

KERRY. I won't if I can help it.

*LEE stands with the seesaw between his legs.*

LEE. What sent yer?

*KERRY bounces, trying to make the seesaw go up and down, but LEE stops it.*

KERRY. All yer doing is putting more stuff on yer list. Yer must want to be disappointed.

*LEE smiles.*

LEE. What yer here for when yer still at school in Dormanstown? I know where you go.

KERRY. You'll know why I go then, won't yer.

LEE. Am I as aggressive as you?

KERRY. Don't ask me. I'm not bothered and I care less, big head.

LEE. I bet you do care, Kerry. I live up the road. Three doors along. Your mam talked to our mam. Your father's gone to prison. Your mam asked our mam if we could make friends with you. It's not a dump by the way.

KERRY. Me mam didn't do that.

LEE. She did or how else would I know.

KERRY. She doesn't have the wherewithal, does she. I live with me dad. I did live with me dad.

LEE. What's he inside for?

KERRY. Does it matter to you?

LEE. Probably not.

KERRY. Theft on a colossal scale, so the judge said. What yer asking us for if you know?

LEE. I didn't know that in particular.

*KERRY jumps off the seesaw. LEE falls with a thump.*

KERRY. Watch yer bollocks, if you've got any.

*She goes to the swing, takes her geography file out of the carrier bag, and sits.*

LEE. You could be more pleasant for a start off. It doesn't cost anything.

KERRY. I wouldn't give you the benefit.

*KERRY looks through the file.*

LEE. I'm Lee, in case yer want to know.

KERRY. What would I want to know owt off you for? I'm not affected.

*LEE looks at the sun. He jumps up and goes to the wall. He looks at the sun again. KERRY turns to see what he is doing.*

Yer mad, you.

LEE. You'll see something in a few seconds when the sun goes a bit more. Yer know the Methodist hall before it burnt down?

*KERRY looks.*

It's got to drop another inch above that.

*KERRY looks at the file.*

You're going to miss it.

KERRY. There's nowt to miss, far as I'm aware.

*KERRY turns to look at the wall.*

*A piece of graffiti, that wasn't there before, begins to stand out . It is 'Lee Is King Rat' in red paint. As the sun gets to exactly the right angle, it becomes like a hologram written on the air.*

LEE. See it?

KERRY. Yeh. Is that you?

LEE. Yeh. It's only an optical illusion.

*The graffiti goes as quickly as it came.*

I told yer. Yer didn't believe us, did yer?

KERRY. It's not my fault. How am I supposed to know. It's not that clever.

LEE. It is. Could you arrange it to happen?

KERRY. I wouldn't want to. What's the point. Anyone could do that for a kick off easily.

LEE. What sort of paint would you use then?

KERRY. I wouldn't use paint.

*They look at one another.*

All right, you win, I'll let yer tell us how it works.

LEE. No. Why should I?

KERRY. Go on.

LEE. It's for me to know and you to find out.

LEE *goes to the swings.*

Ask us if I like you.

KERRY. D'you like me?

LEE. Yeh. Ask us if I really fancy you.

KERRY. D'you really fancy me?

LEE. Yeh.

KERRY. I wondered why you were hanging about, messing around, talking to us.

LEE. You look good. You look fantastic.

*He moves the carrier bag and sits on the swing.*

KERRY. Don't think yer getting nothing.

LEE. What am I after?

KERRY. Yer'll get nothing out of us in a hurry.

LEE *moves the swing. He wraps it around* KERRY*'s swing so that the two sets of chains become intertwined. They kiss for a few moments.* KERRY *pushes him away.*

That's enough. You've got a tongue like a ferret.

KERRY *slips off the seat.* LEE *is left swinging about as the chains unravel.*

For a kick off, yer breaking the law with us.

LEE. How come?

KERRY. I'm fifteen, clever dick.

LEE. I don't see any police. I didn't make you do owt or anywhere near make you do owt.

KERRY. I never said yer did.

*They look at one another.*

Me mam's poorly with it. Yer all the same you lot.

LEE. Who is?

KERRY. Lads are. I don't go in for it meself.

LEE. Say something friendly, Kerry. Surprise me.

KERRY. I wouldn't give you that much pleasure. You know the trouble with lads?

LEE. No.

KERRY. All of you think yer nearly unique.

LEE. Yer know your trouble?

KERRY. Don't bother, swollen brains.

LEE. Yer not generous enough to be worth the trouble yer causing.

KERRY. It must take one to know one, I reckon.

LEE. I don't enjoy trouble, by the way. It's about the last thing I enjoy.

KERRY. You must be nearly unique then, is all I can say.

LEE. You can't be nearly unique.

KERRY. You are, Lee.

LEE. Yer either unique or yer not.

> KERRY *pauses for a second.*

KERRY. It's only a leg pull, clever clogs. I'm only pulling your leg. Yer take everything dead serious.

> *Silence.*

What?

> KERRY *pauses.*

You'll only let us down. Lads always do. It's always the same. I don't even blame you.

LEE. I reckon there's nothing means anything to you, something of the sort.

> *Silence.*

KERRY. What?

> LEE *gets off the swing. He goes to her.*

LEE. I meant what I said before.

> *He rubs his nose on her nose.* KERRY *kisses him.*

> EWAN PEACOCK *comes on. He is twenty three years old, thin and bony with sharp, spiky features and very short hair. He is wearing jeans and carrying a tee shirt. He has a football, though not a full-size one.*

EWAN. Now then, our kid.

LEE. Where've you been?

EWAN. Playing footy.

LEE. Who with like?

EWAN. Dean and all them lot.

LEE. Oh.

EWAN. I was hat trick boy twice. Scored six so I got to keep Dean's ball. Good eh?

LEE. Did yer?

EWAN. Yeh. I would've had nine, but it's a waste of energy. I've left him crying into his feet like at the dazzling brilliance of us.

LEE. What did you do?

EWAN. He saved me best ever penalty. What was I meant to do? I floored him and took me ball away.

EWAN *looks at her.*

Are you Kerry?

KERRY. Does it make a difference to yer?

LEE. This is me brother Ewan.

EWAN *throws the ball at* LEE*'s head and catches it as it comes back.*

EWAN. Yer've not been slow, our kid. You want to keep a careful eye on him, pet.

*He plays with one of his nipples.*

He's known as Phil the philanderer. He's a right Don Juan. You'd be better with me.

KERRY. What makes yer think that?

EWAN. I'm the sophisticated one of us.

KERRY. Yer fooling me already.

EWAN *throws the ball at* KERRY*'s head and catches it again.*

EWAN. Anything could happen round here to a little lass like you. We eat lasses for breakfast. Don't we?

LEE. Yeh.

KERRY. Does he think he's summat special or am I getting the wrong idea.

LEE. It's only our Ewan. It's how he is.

EWAN *moves to throw the ball.* KERRY *goes to catch it.* EWAN *doesn't throw it, then he does. He catches the ball as it comes back off* KERRY*'s head.*

KERRY. Clever clog brains. Lousy prick. Yer worse than him.

LEE. No, I'm not, I'm cleverer than him.

KERRY. Don't defend us in a hurry, I wouldn't.

LEE. He doesn't mean nothing, Kerry.

EWAN. Yes, I do.

EWAN *puts down the ball. He goes to the seesaw. He jumps on and starts to walk along it.* KERRY *kicks the ball away.* LEE *goes after it before it disappears.*

Yer'll regret that later. Yer a spirited little thing. How's yer mam?

KERRY. Is it any of your business?

EWAN. I might make it my business.

LEE *comes back with the ball.*

KERRY. What did you do that for?

EWAN. Has she still got them hundreds of cockroaches?

KERRY. I wouldn't know.

EWAN. She can't have else you would. You could hear them scuttling about when I was in there once. There was so much racket from 'em you was nearly deaf with it. Those are dirty creatures to have in your home.

EWAN *jumps off the seesaw. He grabs hold of* KERRY *and pushes her arm hard up her back.*

KERRY. Ow. Bloody ow.

EWAN. Whose ball is it?

KERRY. Yours.

EWAN. Thank you. Say thank you as well.

KERRY. Thanks.

EWAN *lets her go.*

Don't you say owt. I wouldn't, I must say.

LEE. He's only playing a bit.

EWAN. I'm only playing with yer a lot. Anyone would think you'd got reasons to be aggrieved.

EWAN *dribbles the ball, though he is not very good.*

LEE *looks at* KERRY.

LEE. He's all right after a while. He doesn't mean most of it.

KERRY. He didn't half hurt us because of you.

EWAN *looks off.*

EWAN. Dean, yer moronic cripple.

*He kicks the ball back.*

That lad's a parasite. Satisfied, our kid?

LEE. Yeh.

EWAN *jumps on the seesaw. He walks along it.*

EWAN. Get off with our Lee and you'll find he don't like trouble in any shape or form. Tell us I'm wrong, our lad.

LEE. Something like it, yeh.

EWAN. Kerry.

KERRY *ignores him.*

Kerry.

KERRY. What?

EWAN. Yer from Dormanstown?

KERRY. You know more about me than I do.

EWAN. I go up to Dormanstown and Redcar sometimes. There's a lot of interesting stuff up there, a fair amount of drugs knocking about.

KERRY *ignores him.*

Sulk all year. No one's going to sulk along with yer. You've inherited yer mam in yer.

KERRY. I can tell you're a moron.

EWAN. I preferred you when you were quiet.

LEE *is embarrassed. He goes away. He sits on one of the swings.* EWAN *looks at* KERRY. *He leaps off the seesaw, going in her direction.* KERRY *flinches, but only slightly.* EWAN *goes to the other swing, jumps onto the seat and stands on it.*

She gives you a roller coaster ride, don't she.

LEE. Yeh.

KERRY. Do I have to wait till next week?

LEE. What for?

KERRY. If you don't know now, yer never will. Yer not as good as yer promise, I know that much.

EWAN. Yer meant to be defending her, our kid.

KERRY. Yer brother's got it in one.

EWAN. I'd watch her closely. She's trouble and bit extra.

KERRY. He watches us anyway, since he fancies us rotten.

EWAN. Do yer?

LEE. Course not.

EWAN. She'd curdle milk soon as look at it.

LEE. I've told you not.

KERRY. I don't fancy him, so there.

EWAN. D'you fancy us?

KERRY. I can't ever see me being that desperate.

EWAN. I'm glad I'm appreciated. Kerry. It must be dead different living in the country.

   KERRY *goes to the seesaw and sits.*

KERRY. Yer right about the dead bit.

EWAN. It's a village if yer want to compare it. Dormanstown is a hole.

KERRY. It might be to you.

EWAN. All them lousy, disease-ridden flats, full of lousy, disease-ridden people.

KERRY. I thought yer went up there?

EWAN. I do. It's how I know I'm right. I don't go for pleasure, pet. I go to deal. What's your school?

KERRY. Our Lady of the Sacred Heart of Dormanstown, or something. What's it to you?

EWAN. When you stop taking the piss, I'll tell yer that I know it well. There's more good stuff floating about in there than books. You want to be happier than miserable.

KERRY. Why?

EWAN. There's fields round here.

KERRY. Am I meant to walk across them?

EWAN. Yes, and enjoy it on a summer's evening like this.

KERRY. Yer don't take yer own advice, is all I can say.

HAZEL *and* DENNIS *enter.* DENNIS *is wearing black jeans and a black shirt.* HAZEL *is in a skirt.*

HAZEL. I might have known you two'd be getting her into trouble, if she's not put both feet in it already.

KERRY. Shuv off, Mam.

HAZEL. A slip of a lass and she doesn't know how to have a gooder time than this. If yer can't have a good time when yer a baby, when can yer have? Don't all shout at once.

HAZEL *sits beside* KERRY.

Sorry I wasn't in, petal. I've had more pressing things on me mind. Dennis had some money he wanted to spend in the Royal Oak. How could I let him down?

DENNIS *is doing his best to stand upright.*

DENNIS. If she's a slip of thing, which she isn't, leave the slip of a thing alone. She speaks with forked tongue does that one, lads. Boys, it's nice to meet you.

EWAN. You get off home, before you lose all your dignity.

DENNIS. There's a quiet one as well. I like silence. It's thoughtful. You and me, we'll get on. What's yer name?

LEE. Lee.

DENNIS. I can tell yer going to be intelligent. Keep it while I'm sober. See yer, Lee.

LEE. Yeh, see yer.

DENNIS *goes to* HAZEL. *He takes her hand and tries to pull her up.* HAZEL *kisses* KERRY*'s cheek.*

HAZEL. I like you, love. You're the good in me.

KERRY. There's nowt good in you, Mam. Anythings that's good, I got from me dad.

DENNIS. Come on, leave the cow alone.

HAZEL. She's my baby. I'm going to keep my baby forever and see she's safe like mammies do.

DENNIS *pulls* HAZEL *to her feet.*

DENNIS. Yer not going to change her. She's a foregone conclusion that one is.

HAZEL. I've tried my bestest with her, Dennis. No one could have done more apart from Jesus. You know something? She's taken the life out of me that cow has. I've talked to The Lord. The Lord knows what I've done. Jesus forgives everybody.

HAZEL *and* DENNIS *leave.*

*The light has begun to go and the shadows lengthen. It is a beautiful, idyllic evening.*

EWAN *gets the swing going. He goes higher and higher.*

LEE *is looking at* KERRY.

KERRY. What yer looking at, goggle eyes? Seen something yer don't like?

LEE. No.

*He looks down.*

It's more the opposite.

KERRY. Yer talking to us? I wouldn't waste yer breath, yer've nowt to say that I want to hear.

LEE. I said it's more the opposite.

EWAN *jumps off the swing as it reaches the top of the arc. He lands near* KERRY.

EWAN. Kissy kissy.

KERRY. Go and fancy yerself, no one else does.

EWAN. Give us a long lingering kiss.

KERRY. You know what you are. Yer completely pathetic in my opinion. At least yer brother's got no scruples. At least yer know where yer are with him. Is he frightened of yer or is he just scared?

EWAN. Are you frightened of us or are you just scared, kid?

LEE. Course not.

KERRY. Does he ever say what he means?

EWAN. D'you ever say what you mean, Lee?

LEE. Course I do.

EWAN *looks at her. He plays with his nipples.*

KERRY. Neither of yous is funny. I'd laugh more if you were six feet under.

KERRY *gets up. She goes to the swing and sits.*

Don't think I like yer.

LEE. No.

KERRY. Yer a bigger idiot than I thought. Give us yer excuse, if yer've got one.

LEE. I can't stand this place.

KERRY. Is that it? Why didn't yer defend us when I said it was a dump, since I was right to start off with?

LEE *shrugs.*

LEE. You always stick up for where yer live, don't yer. I'm only like you.

KERRY. If that's a compliment yer a bit late with it.

LEE. Yeh, it was meant to be.

EWAN *goes to* KERRY. *He takes hold of the chains of the swing so that she can't get away.* KERRY *stands up. She kisses* EWAN *full on the mouth for quite a long time.*

LEE *gets up and goes to the seesaw.*

KERRY *pushes* EWAN *off.*

KERRY. That's plenty.

EWAN. What?

KERRY. You've had enough fun to be going on with.

*She sits on the swing.* EWAN *sits on the other one. He pulls her near so that their faces are close together.*

EWAN. Yer crafty as sneaky can be.

KERRY. Yer not wrong, Lee's brother. Yer like it.

EWAN. I might.

KERRY. Yes, yer do. Yer'd hate it if I wasn't crafty.

EWAN. Yer know no limits.

KERRY. What limits are those?

EWAN. I'll have to find out.

EWAN *pulls her closer.*

Anything you want, you tell us. It's yours before you ask. That is whilst I'm with yer. Other times you'll be on your own.

KERRY *kisses him.*

LEE *is drawing an imaginary picture on the ground with his finger.*

KERRY. Will you do us a favour?

EWAN. Any favour you want.

KERRY. It's a big one.

EWAN. I can't do it if yer don't tell us.

KERRY. You know Dennis the menace?

EWAN. In the comic?

KERRY. The bloke me mam was with.

EWAN. Him?

KERRY. Yeh.

EWAN. I didn't mind him.

KERRY. Will yer give him a going over, crack him one for us, rough him up a bit, give him a scare? Yer could put him in hospital for the night if yer can be bothered.

EWAN. What's he done?

KERRY. It don't matter what he's done.

EWAN. It's a small favour, pet. It's no skin of my nose. I make yer the promise that he won't forget it. Is he getting his end away at your mam's?

KERRY. Yeh.

EWAN. She's been done that often it must be liking putting it into a pair of old shoes.

EWAN *kisses her.*

KERRY. Yer know something, Lee's brother, yer the best there is in the whole world.

## Scene Three

*The living room. That night.*

*The room is in a mess again from the evening. A yellow light is spilling in from the lamp post outside, illuminating* KERRY *who is by the window looking out. She is still. She is wearing a nightdress and has bare feet. A whirling, blue police light is flashing round the room, which is eerily silent.*

HAZEL *comes in. She is wearing the negligee and shoes. She has some rosary beads.*

KERRY *turns.*

KERRY. What's gone off, Mam?

HAZEL. It's Dennis the menace.

KERRY. What about him? He's all right, isn't he?

HAZEL. No.

KERRY. What's wrong with him? What's right with him more like.

HAZEL. He's only dead as a door nail in the playground yer go to.

KERRY. He isn't. He isn't. Get out.

HAZEL. He is, love.

KERRY. He's good riddance to bad rubbish, is all I can say.

HAZEL. You shouldn't say that.

   HAZEL*'s hands are shaking. She plays with the rosary.*

KERRY. Any how, Mam, he'll be back in soon.

HAZEL. I've seen him by the swings. If he's alive it's a miracle. He only went out for a packet of fags.

KERRY. Yer getting yourself all fidgety over nothing.

HAZEL. I am fidgety.

KERRY. You've seen wrong. You know how you get. I bet it's not even Dennis.

   *A slight pause.*

HAZEL. I'm sure I saw him. He was covered in blood. His face was any road.

KERRY. No.

HAZEL. Yes.

KERRY. Why?

HAZEL. I don't know why.

KERRY *looks down and back up.*

KERRY. Are you absolutely sure it was Dennis?

HAZEL. I know Dennis when I see him, baby, don't I?

KERRY. Yeh, I suppose so.

*A slight pause.*

I don't know what's gone off then.

HAZEL *pulls out a dining chair and sits at the table.*

HAZEL. I don't know if I'm going to get over this.

KERRY. Yer will do, Mam.

HAZEL. Not quickly I won't. He was all right was Dennis when yer got used to him.

KERRY. Yer only knew him a day and a bit.

HAZEL. It was enough to know he was generous. He couldn't do harm if he tried.

*A slight pause.*

It's not right what's gone off.

KERRY *goes to her.*

KERRY. Don't get upset.

HAZEL. I am upset. What else am I meant to be?

KERRY *finds it difficult to touch her mother. She sort of pats her back.*

KERRY. Yer'll get over it.

HAZEL. I don't want to get over it.

KERRY *sits on a dining chair.*

KERRY. What was he like, Mam?

HAZEL. I'm not thinking about it.

KERRY. Was he bad?

HAZEL. He could have been more politer could Dennis, but he didn't deserve bad things. He was going to take us on holiday.

KERRY. Where?

HAZEL. I don't know.

KERRY. I meant was he bad in the playground.

HAZEL. Yes. I reckon someone knocked him senseless, then he was dead in a second.

*KERRY glances down and back up. She sees* DENNIS *enter. His hair is wet, and he is dressed in an off-white, towelling bathrobe. He is carrying some tools and an old tap together with a new one still in its packaging.* KERRY *watches him go to the sofa and sit down.*

KERRY. He isn't dead, Mam. Yer being daft.

HAZEL. I don't know who is then. It's some unlucky sod.

KERRY. It can't be. Yer not listening to us.

HAZEL. I know what I saw. He was going to bring all his belongings round once he'd mentioned us to his wife. I hope you feel a bit guilty about it.

KERRY. I don't.

HAZEL. You should, it's only sensible.

KERRY. What for? It's not my fault.

HAZEL. He went on and on about being a good dad to you.

KERRY. He'll say anything as long as it gets him a favour.

*KERRY glances at* Dennis. *He is looking at the old tap and reading the instructions on the new one.*

You know how he tells lies, Mam.

HAZEL. He didn't.

KERRY. I'm telling yer he does for certain. He lies non-stop. He's gone and forgotten what the truth is. You don't know about him.

HAZEL. You want to wash your mouth out like I was made as a kid.

KERRY *glances at* DENNIS. *He is taking the new tap out of its Cellophane packet.*

HAZEL *puts the rosary on the table. She finds some cigarettes in a pocket in the negligee, and lights one.*

KERRY. Yer could give us one.

HAZEL. Buy yer own. You shouldn't smoke anyway. I don't know what I'm going to do.

*A slight pause.*

Take one if yer must. You'll only make me feel guilty. Yer always have.

*A slight pause.*

What's up with yer?

KERRY. I don't want one.

HAZEL. I was only kidding. Have one.

KERRY. No.

HAZEL. What's wrong with yer?

KERRY. Nothing.

HAZEL *smokes. Her hand is shaking.*

HAZEL. If you want me to feel bad, I'm not about to, Kerry. I wish I'd been firmer with you from the start. I'd do a lot of things different if another chance came along. It's my fault you've walked all over me. The guilt I've got inside has a lot to answer for. It's let you do as you please and not much else.

KERRY. I never do as I please, Mam.

HAZEL. You give a good impression. You're happy, aren't you?

KERRY. Of course I'm not.

HAZEL. Oh. I thought you was.

KERRY. I'd rather be dead than be us sometimes.

HAZEL. Why didn't you tell me?

KERRY. Could I?

HAZEL. I'm your mam, pet.

KERRY. I didn't know I could.

HAZEL *smokes.*

HAZEL. This has done for me a bit. I wish I'd not gone out. I was only being nosey.

KERRY *glances at* DENNIS. *He is taking the old tap apart and assembling the new one with a monkey-wrench, pliers and a screwdriver. He is not very practical.*

KERRY. Was there anyone else in the playground, Mam?

HAZEL. No, only Dennis the menace. Give us the ashtray.

KERRY *passes the ashtray. She glances at* DENNIS.

KERRY. He can't be dead, can he, Mam?

HAZEL. He can because he is. I'd got some hopes of us being a normal family. When I was your age I thought good things would happen easy as me thinking it. Do you?

KERRY. What?

HAZEL. Think that.

KERRY. I didn't hear what you said.

HAZEL. What's new.

KERRY. What, Mam?

HAZEL. Nothing's new. You don't ever listen.

HAZEL *touches her ears.*

I use these things God gave me. Dennis would be alive if it weren't for you.

KERRY. What's that about when it's at home?

HAZEL. You was in his way.

KERRY. I was not.

HAZEL. He went out for a bit of peace for five minutes and got himself murdered for his trouble.

KERRY. Don't yer want us ever?

HAZEL. I want you to be tidier.

KERRY. I am. I am, aren't I?

HAZEL. You don't seem it to me.

*A slight pause.*

I'm only being honest with yer.

*A slight pause.*

Have I said something wrong?

KERRY *shakes her head.*

I must have done else why are you carrying on.

*A slight pause.*

If I'd gone on as you do half the time, I wouldn't have lived.

KERRY. Yer could like us a tiny bit. You could pretend even if you didn't.

HAZEL. I do like you. When have I said the opposite?

KERRY. Just now.

HAZEL. I didn't. Yer imagining it.

KERRY. I'm not. I know what I heard, Mam.

HAZEL. I didn't say anything of the sort. I've always said, you're my flesh and blood. It's the reason why I've always been scrupulous with yer.

KERRY *gets up. She pulls out a dining chair, one that is further away from her mother, and sits on it.*

Don't have a tantrum. I'm not in the mood.

HAZEL *pushes the cigarette packet towards her.*

Have one of these. There's a murder going on, we're bound to be a bit tense.

KERRY *pushes the packet back. She puts her forehead on the table.*

There's nothing to see down there. If I'd acted up as bad as you, me mam wouldn't have spoken to us for a month.

KERRY. Are you jealous?

HAZEL. Jealous of what, pet?

KERRY. Me.

HAZEL *smokes.*

HAZEL. Why? I don't think so. I know so.

KERRY. I want you to tell us why you don't love us.

HAZEL. Don't start that again. We've been through it once.

KERRY. You have. I haven't.

HAZEL *smokes.*

HAZEL. I do love you.

KERRY. You've got a funny way of showing it, Mam.

HAZEL. I show it in my own way. Isn't it good enough for yer?

KERRY. You tell me.

HAZEL. It musn't be since yer carrying on. What d'you want, Kerry?

KERRY. I want you to care about us.

HAZEL. Yer think I don't when I do. I do all sorts yer never hear about. I asked Lee and Ewan to look out for yer for one thing.

KERRY. Fat lot of good that was.

HAZEL. Watch Ewan, pet. He's dangerous. He's got a screw loose.

HAZEL *smokes.*

Yer could look at us.

KERRY *looks up at her mother.*

KERRY. What for, Mam?

HAZEL. I do my best.

HAZEL *smokes.*

KERRY. D'you think I love you?

HAZEL. I don't know. I haven't given it a thought.

HAZEL *stubs out the cigarette. She picks up the rosary. Her hands are shaking.*

Lee's the better of them, love. Go with him. He's a good lad. He's been inside, which maybe he'll tell you about.

He's done time in a young offenders' prison, but he isn't bad. I've always liked Lee. Yer listening to me, pet?

KERRY. Yeh.

HAZEL. Only it's important.

KERRY. What's up with yer, Mam?

*HAZEL is trying to keep her hands still and for the most part succeeding.*

HAZEL. It comes on us sometimes. It was nearly coming before. It'll go in a minute.

*HAZEL's hands become still.*

I went to the doctor and he gave me tablets for me nerves, as if that had owt to do with it. It does I suppose.

*HAZEL lights a cigarette and pushes the packet towards KERRY, who picks it up. She gets up and sits on the chair she was sitting on before. She puts the cigarettes near her mother. She plucks up the courage and takes hold of her mother's hands.*

Don't. I don't like yer touching us.

*KERRY continues.*

I said don't paw me.

*KERRY takes her hands away. She sits back.*

KERRY. Sorry. I won't touch yer again. I couldn't be less bothered. See if I worry.

*HAZEL smokes. Her hand begins to shake.*

HAZEL. It's too hot and sweaty. You get on me nerves, sometimes, you do. You think you can do owt and get away with it. I couldn't as a kid, so why should you? You don't make the best of it like the rest of us has to. You think you're special.

KERRY. I don't.

HAZEL. It's written all over yer, pet. You want to open your eyes. You're not going to achieve nothing.

KERRY. I will. I bet I am.

HAZEL. I'm not getting at yer.

KERRY. You are.

HAZEL. I must love you enough to tell you the truth. It'd be far more easier for me to fib to yer, love. I've done everything in my God given power for you. I hope yer won't do much wrong.

*HAZEL holds the cigarette and runs her hand through her hair.*

KERRY. Careful, Mam.

HAZEL. What?

KERRY. You'll burn yourself.

*HAZEL smokes.*

I can achieve lots of stuff if I try.

HAZEL. You'll need more luck than I had, love. I've answered some of your queries. Have I?

KERRY. Yeh.

HAZEL. I'm a bad person, I know that.

KERRY. You're not.

HAZEL. Generally speaking. Not now. Some good's got to come of it.

KERRY. What?

HAZEL. Tonight. Some good's got to come out between us.

*KERRY glances at DENNIS.*

*LEE appears outside. He taps on the glass. KERRY goes to the window and opens it.*

LEE. Have yer seen our Ewan anywhere?

*KERRY glances at DENNIS. She shakes her head.*

KERRY. No.

LEE. Yer know what's gone off?

KERRY. We'd have to be even dafter than you, wouldn't we?

LEE. Yeh. They've just shoved him in a bag a minute ago.

HAZEL. Tell him to come in.

KERRY. Me mam says d'you want to come in?

HAZEL. The door's on the latch.

LEE *goes.* KERRY *shuts the window just as* DENNIS *is getting up. She sees him go out with the taps and tools.*

KERRY. You should go to bed, Mam.

HAZEL. How can I go to bed? It's too hot for one thing.

KERRY. You might sleep.

HAZEL. How? I've a fat chance.

LEE *comes in. He has bare feet. He is wearing jeans and a baggy tee shirt.*

*The police light stops flashing.*

Put the light on, pet. We may as well be up since we are.

LEE. I'll do it, Mrs Cooper.

LEE *turns on the electric light. The room is bright and bland. This time it is* LEE *who sees* DENNIS *enter.* DENNIS *is dressed in black jeans. He has a newspaper tucked under his chin. He is putting on and fastening his black shirt.* LEE *mutters.*

KERRY. What?

LEE. Nothing. I didn't say anything.

KERRY. Are you feeling bad about something?

LEE. Are you?

KERRY. No.

HAZEL. Is the party in full swing, Lee?

LEE. Half the road is out. More than half the road, Mrs Cooper.

HAZEL. I hope everyone's getting their money's-worth, are they?

LEE. Yeh.

KERRY *brushes* LEE*'s arm. She sits at the table.* LEE *glances at* DENNIS. DENNIS *is on the sofa reading the paper.*

Who found him, have you any idea like?

HAZEL. Dean did.

LEE. I thought it was Dean might have done it. Has he? He's handcuffed in a police van at the moment, and not very happy about it. Sheryl's screaming blue murder at them.

HAZEL. It wasn't Dean.

LEE. How d'you know?

HAZEL. I just do. Sit down, Lee, yer making the place look untidy.

LEE *pulls out a dining chair and sits.*

My money's on your Ewan.

LEE. Yer what?

HAZEL. Keep yer hair on. I'm only kidding yer, Lee. I'm not getting involved. You lot shouldn't. All of us should keep out of it.

LEE *looks at* KERRY. KERRY *brushes a finger across her lips.* LEE *glances at* DENNIS.

LEE. What happened?

KERRY. Me mam went out to look for him when he didn't come back for hours on end.

HAZEL *is holding the cigarette with her head resting on her hand.*

HAZEL. The police was just arriving. In about a minute there was police everywhere. Dean had dialled 999 on one of them dodgy mobile phones that's been going around in the pubs. He was slung in a police car and nicked for his pains. It's not him, it's someone else. Why would he ring up an ambulance if he's done it.

KERRY. Mam.

HAZEL. What?

KERRY. You'll be alight soon.

HAZEL *smokes. Her hand is shaking.* KERRY *picks up the cigarettes.*

KERRY. Mam?

HAZEL. I've told yer ten times.

KERRY *takes a cigarette. She offers them to* LEE. LEE *takes one.* HAZEL *lights their cigarettes.*

LEE. They'll come for us almost certain.

KERRY. They won't.

LEE. They will. They have to enjoy themselves once a month.

HAZEL. They always come for yer Lee, don't they? It's as sure as eggs is eggs. Why do they always come for yer dad, love? It might be the countryside, but the police are no different to Dormanstown.

KERRY. What did yer do?

LEE. It doesn't matter. I didn't mean to do it. I had a fracas with a schoolkid once.

HAZEL. You broke his neck, didn't yer?

LEE. Yes. Unfortunately for me. I suppose more unfortunately for him actually. I pushed him off a wall. It was an accident. He overbalanced. They said I pushed him, but I didn't really. I got four years for it. I was guilty of GBH with intent. I didn't intend. They said I should have foresaw the consequences. I was fifteen. The boy was eleven. A lot was made of that in court with the judge and the jury and everything. That's what swung it against us. Also I looked older by the time I came to court. The lad was in a wheelchair which didn't help us. All the sympathy was bound to be with him. And when my antecedence was read out I'd got shoplifting charges, and cautions and all that. The judge said he'd no choice but to send me down. He said I was on a slippery slope and a very dangerous young man. I wasn't a young man. I was a kid who'd just done something on the spur of the moment for no reason. The only person who cared was Freya. Freya came to court with us every day. They sent me mam away for shouting at the little boy when he was giving his evidence. The judge told the jury they had to disregard her impudence. How could they? He didn't when he sentenced me, after he'd read all the reports. I could tell he didn't like us, he made it very clear. He ignored the psychiatrist who said a long prison sentence wasn't the best option for us. I was already being bullied in Deerbolt, so I know what he meant. It was me who'd told him anyway. I told him I'd been raped by two bully boys in the showers, one after the other, and one who just watched and didn't do it. I told him I wasn't coping at all well.

*The doorbell rings.*

HAZEL. They've taken their time I musn't say, considering they were coming straight off. You've been with us all evening, Lee.

LEE*'s legs are twitching from the balls of his feet up.*

KERRY. Who is it, Mam?

LEE. Me mam knows I've been with her.

HAZEL. Which d'you want?

LEE. She's been out of it most of the night pissed. When she's not been out of it she's been asleep. I've been with you like.

HAZEL. We didn't watch tele –

*She gets up and picks up the TV Times.*

Apart from E.T. Lee?

LEE. Yeh, I've seen it. I saw it tonight.

HAZEL. Have you, Kerry?

KERRY. I've watched it loads of times. It's not believable.

HAZEL. You go.

KERRY. I'm not going.

HAZEL. Go on. Tell them I'm not thinking about it. Tell them we're all too upset.

*The doorbell rings.*

It's none of their business anyhow. They'll only want to know about his lousy wife. Let them wait and find out he's married to her. They make more problems than they solve them lot.

## Scene Four

*A cornfield. Dawn, several hours later.*

*There is a low mist settled between the rows of almost ripe barley. A pale, watery sunlight is catching hold of the heads of corn that are poking out of the white field.*

LEE *enters walking between two of the rows. He has put on a jumper. He calls.*

LEE. Ewan.

KERRY *enters between another two rows. She is wearing her school uniform and has the carrier bag.*

KERRY. It's a needle in a haystack all this.

LEE *stops.*

LEE. You go.

KERRY. No thanks. D'you want me to?

LEE. It's up to you.

KERRY. I'd only be miles too soon. I'll probably bump into him outside school after what he said. It'd be just my luck.

LEE. Yeh.

KERRY. You're creepy you, I've decided.

LEE. Why?

KERRY. Ewan. I can't tell what you're thinking like I can other idiots. I'm trusting me mam's right at the moment. There's a first time for everything.

LEE. Right about what?

KERRY. She likes you for some reason. It makes you unique.

LEE. I like her sometimes, when she's not acting up.

KERRY. More than you like me?

LEE. No.

KERRY. Phew, that's a relief.

LEE. Don't be sarcastic.

KERRY. What's that about when it's at home?

LEE. It's when you mock someone.

KERRY. I know what it is. I'm not a halfwit you know.

LEE *kicks the mist.*

You're quite shy you, I've realised.

LEE *smiles.*

LEE. I feel like I've been pushed through a hedge backwards.

KERRY. Yeh, great minds think alike.

*Silence.*

What?

LEE. I didn't say anything.

KERRY. You were going to.

LEE. I wasn't.

KERRY. I bet you were.

LEE. What was I going to say?

KERRY. Why should I tell you? People are always telling me I'm thick. I've heard it so often I don't care any more if it's true. Don't say anything then, I wouldn't.

LEE. All right I won't.

KERRY. Yer could say something. Yer could say it isn't true.

LEE. It isn't.

KERRY. I might believe you if I didn't had to drag it out of you.

*A slight pause.*

Lee, I like you a lot. I wish I'd never mentioned nothing now.

LEE. Thanks.

KERRY. You're a slippery fish suddenly.

LEE. I don't mean to be.

KERRY. Blame me if you want. I would. I am.

LEE. I don't like it one bit, Kerry.

KERRY. D'you think I do?

LEE. I don't know.

KERRY. Cross my heart and hope to die, I don't.

LEE. Why did you say it?

KERRY. He touched us up. He had it coming.

LEE. Ewan touched you up. What's the difference?

KERRY. Are you jealous?

LEE. I'm not jealous.

KERRY. I only did it to make you jealous.

LEE. You succeeded.

KERRY. It's a right mess.

LEE. Yeh, it is.

*A slight pause.*

KERRY. It's my fault, I know that.

LEE. It's my fault for keeping me mouth shut.

KERRY. You sat there like a dummy.

LEE. Don't rub it in. You know what makes it worse, Kerry?

KERRY. No.

LEE. I knew he'd do it.

KERRY. I didn't. I can't help what I hoped for. You've got to hope for something, otherwise what's the point?

*One of* LEE*'s knees is twitching. He puts his hand on it to hold it still. He shivers.*

LEE. I'm freezing cold.

KERRY. D'you want my blazer for a bit?

LEE. No.

KERRY. What's up?

LEE. I'm just chilly.

KERRY *goes to him.*

KERRY. You look a bit funny. You look a lot funny. You've got a sweat on. I want to be a nurse.

KERRY *puts her palm on* LEE*'s forehead.*

EWAN *comes on. He has put on a leather jacket.*

EWAN. Now then kiddoes.

KERRY. I told you to crack him one.

EWAN. Keep yer hair on. What's up with yer? I did crack him one. I put him in hospital for yer, didn't I?

KERRY. I didn't want him put in hospital.

EWAN. Well, there's memories and there's memories, pet. It's the last favour yer getting out of me

KERRY. I wish like hell he was.

EWAN *takes a packet of cigarettes out of his jacket pocket and lights one.*

You haven't the foggiest what's gone off, have yer? He's only dead.

EWAN. He's not. I'm wise to that one.

KERRY. Tell yer big brother what's gone on all night.

EWAN. He wasn't dead when I left him. He was in the peak of health. He was nodding like a Trojan when I told him he would be dead if he said owt about us.

KERRY. He only swallowed his tongue and choked, so everyone's saying any road up.

EWAN. Is it my fault if he's got a tongue?

KERRY. I don't know how you can be you.

EWAN. Easily.

KERRY. I don't know how yer can live with yourself. I couldn't. Yer should have known I didn't mean it. I was only kidding yer. I was having yer on.

EWAN. Great. Oh, great.

KERRY. It was only a lark. Can't yer know when somebody is larking about with yer? Yer warped, yer must be.

*A tear comes into one of* KERRY*'s eyes.*

EWAN. Don't cry.

KERRY. I'm not crying. I wouldn't cry because of you if you paid me a trillion pounds. You haven't been with us. You don't know what we've been through.

LEE. Where've you been all night, our kid?

EWAN. Over at the girlfriend's.

KERRY. He's been questioned because of you.

EWAN. I know that. Tell us news. I knew he would be. Keep yer shirt on. I didn't tell him. He doesn't know anything.

I didn't get him to help us. You're going to be in a coffin before you're any older. You worry far too much.

KERRY. It's all right for you.

EWAN. Have you had their hospitality, Lee?

LEE *shakes his head. He shivers.*

LEE. They questioned us at Kerry's mam's.

EWAN. I know you're innocent, you know you're innocent. You can't get less evidence.

LEE. I said I was with Kerry though. I wasn't.

EWAN. You should have said you were at Freya's. Where were you, puppet brain?

LEE. At home. Only me mam was out of it.

EWAN. What did yer lie for, yer dozy ponce?

LEE. I don't know. I couldn't say Freya's.

KERRY. I know why. We was scared.

EWAN. Yer mam's okay, isn't she, pet?

KERRY. It was her idea, if I can remember properly, which I can't.

EWAN. All's well.

KERRY. You must think you're charmed.

EWAN. I am.

KERRY. You don't charm me much.

EWAN *looks at her.*

EWAN. That's where you're wrong.

KERRY *looks away.*

Sexy bitch.

KERRY *looks at* LEE *out of the corner of her eye.*

KERRY. I don't believe you. You don't even stick up for yourself.

EWAN. You know you like us. Kerry, Kerry.

KERRY. Yer a bit full of yourself for my liking.

EWAN. You'll take that back before a minute's gone by.

KERRY. I'll take nothing back.

EWAN *grabs* KERRY*'s arm and gives her a Chinese burn.*

Yeh, all right.

EWAN *stops.*

EWAN. I'd nearly a minute left.

KERRY. I hate you more than anyone else.

EWAN. You don't.

KERRY. You think yer tough.

EWAN. I don't think.

KERRY. I know yer don't.

EWAN. Clever, Kerry.

KERRY. I'm cleverer than you any day of the week.

EWAN. You'd be surprised.

KERRY. The day you surprise me I'll know I'm an idiot.

EWAN *takes hold of her arm.*

If you Chinese us again –

EWAN. What?

KERRY. Something. I don't know. I'll set him on yer.

EWAN. Yer rude to him, yer rude to me, pet. Have you got that?

KERRY. Yeh, I suppose so.

EWAN. Good.

LEE. Leave her be, Ewan.

KERRY. Blimey. Miracles never cease. He disappears when you're around. He's lively when yer miles off. It's why I like yer most when yer not here.

LEE. Pack it in, Kerry.

KERRY. I won't.

EWAN. You're all mouth. I love it.

KERRY. You know something, Lee. I bet he pushed the kid off that wall. You never did. He should have been in court. It should have happened to him, all that stuff.

LEE. Give it a rest.

KERRY. Why should I?

EWAN. You'd like it to be me, pet. It'd make you fancy us some more.

EWAN *kisses her full on the mouth.* KERRY *only partly resists.*

*A clock in the town half a mile away begins to chime seven o'clock.*

*When* KERRY *needs to take a breath she pushes* EWAN *off. She goes to* LEE *and kisses him in much the same way as* EWAN *kissed her.*

KERRY. Put that in your pipe and smoke it if you dare.

EWAN. See yer kiddoes.

EWAN *goes.*

KERRY. Who's Freya when she's at home?

FREYA *enters following the path round the field. She is forty eight years old, tall and thin with an unforced dignity. She is wearing a light summer dress and stout shoes which the mist is obscuring. She has a leather holdall with some books in and some bright red flowers that are sticking out of the top.*

LEE *hears someone and turns.*

LEE. Freya. Where are you going?

FREYA. To school.

LEE. You're very early.

FREYA. I thought I'd walk this morning. Aren't you going to introduce me.

LEE. This is Kerry.

FREYA. Hello.

KERRY *mutters.*

KERRY. Why should I say hello to you?

LEE. Don't start.

FREYA. Are you going to school as well?

KERRY. Not round here I'm not. It's a dump.

FREYA *pauses for a second.*

FREYA. I've been thinking about you. You haven't been round for a fortnight or so.

LEE. I've been a bit busy like.

FREYA. Yes, I can see.

LEE. It's not what you think.

LEE *shivers really badly.*

FREYA. You know how it is when I don't see you for a few weeks.

LEE. Yeh.

FREYA *puts down the holdall. The top of it and the flowers stick out of the mist. She goes to* LEE.

FREYA. What's the matter?

LEE. I need a hit.

FREYA. Have you got some?

LEE. Yeh, it's here.

LEE *wanders about, gently scraping his foot through the soil underneath the mist.*

KERRY. You should watch out you. He's my friend.

FREYA. Does she know, Lee? Have you explained? Can I tell her?

LEE. Yeh, she won't say anything. I'm going to shit myself if I don't find it.

FREYA. He became addicted to heroin in prison.

KERRY. Oh. Yeh.  I'll know then, won't I.

LEE. Will yer hold us, Freya.

FREYA *holds him.*

FREYA. What's happened to the methadone?

LEE. I can't use it. It's no good. It's useless.

KERRY. I wondered why we'd come this way.

LEE. Can you look, Kerry. It's here somewhere.

KERRY *looks about.*

KERRY. What am I looking for?

LEE *breaks away from the hold with* FREYA.

LEE. It's the seventh row up from the edge.

LEE *goes to the spot where he's remembered it might be. He kneels down and runs his fingers through the soil underneath the mist. When he brings his hand out he has a small packet of tin foil.*

FREYA. Have you got it?

LEE. Yeh.

LEE *takes a small, red, cellophane tube and a lighter from his pocket. He puts the tube in his mouth. He opens out the tin foil which contains the heroin, and plays the lighter underneath. He inhales the fumes through the tube.*

That reached the spot.

LEE *continues to inhale as the heroin melts.* FREYA *goes to him. She kneels down.*

FREYA. It's better than injecting. Only a little better.

LEE. I used to dig, Kerry.

KERRY. I'm not talking to you. You shouldn't do that. It serves you right if you get punished for it.

LEE. Toot toot toot toot tooot.

KERRY. We're all addicted to something. It doesn't mean we go about doing it.

LEE. Toot toot toot toot tooot.

KERRY. Anyone would think you were a train.

LEE. Toot toot toot toot tooot.

FREYA. It's done, Lee. It's gone.

FREYA *takes the tin foil.* LEE *leans on her with his head on her shoulder and breast bone. She takes the tube out of his mouth and slips it into his pocket. She puts the lighter in his pocket. He is quiet and still.*

LEE. Toot toot toot toot tooot.

FREYA *moves her arm so that she is comfortable. It is almost as if a mother is suckling a child.*

*The sun rises some more, casting light across them and picking them out.*

KERRY. Are you a teacher or something?

FREYA. Yes.

KERRY. You'll find I catch on when it's obvious.

FREYA *smiles.* KERRY *wanders towards her.*

Did you teach him?

FREYA. No, but I wish I had. He wouldn't have been one of my failures, and I've far too many of them.

LEE. Toot toot toot toot tooot.

KERRY. Where d'you go like?

FREYA. Where do I teach?

KERRY. Yeh.

FREYA. In Great Ayton, at the Friends' school.

KERRY. It's a bit funny because he trusts you.

FREYA. Why is it funny?

LEE. Toot toot toot toot tooot.

KERRY. It's not funny. You know what I mean.

FREYA. I don't quite.

KERRY. Give over.

FREYA. Give over what?

KERRY. Yer putting us on the spot. I don't get on with it me. Yer preposterous. It's not fair.

*A slight pause.*

What?

LEE. Toot toot toot toot tooot.

KERRY. Does he always do that?

FREYA. I don't know, Kerry.

KERRY. Oh. I thought you must.

FREYA. No.

KERRY. Give over.

FREYA. I don't know what I'm to stop doing.

KERRY. I've told yer.

FREYA. If I guess I'll get it wrong.

KERRY. Putting us on the spot.

FREYA. Is that all?

KERRY. It's a lot to me, I can tell yer.

FREYA. I get put on the spot all the time.

KERRY. Yer don't.

FREYA. How would you know?

KERRY. You don't seem like it.

FREYA. There's a saying.

KERRY. Yeh, appearances are deceptive.

FREYA. That's it.

LEE. Toot toot toot toot tooot.

FREYA. You said something wasn't fair a minute ago.

KERRY. Yeh.

FREYA. What exactly?

KERRY. I come over jealous sort of thing. Yer brilliant with him, I'll tell yer that for nothing. Yer unique.

*A slight pause.*

What?

FREYA. What what, Kerry?

KERRY. I'm jealous of him if you must know. I'm not jealous of you. It's not fair.

KERRY *walks away.*

FREYA. Where are you going?

KERRY. If you don't like us there's no point in me staying.

FREYA. I don't know you.

KERRY. You could try to like me. It's not asking much. I'm no
worse than him. I'm better than him. I don't take drugs for
a kick off. I've not been raped in prison. It's not fair. You'd
like me if I had. Yer can't just like people for that. Yer have
to look at what they are themselves, and see through them
a bit. There's a lot of me you could see through if you tried.
If you want to know what sort of person I am, I'll tell yer.
I'm always the one who moves over on the pavement.
That's who I am.

*A slight pause.*

What?

FREYA. Is there more?

KERRY. There's tons more. I can't be bothered to tell you
though.

LEE. She's great.

*LEE sits up.*

KERRY. I'm not. Yer just saying that.

*FREYA stands up.*

FREYA. Well.

KERRY. Well what?

FREYA. It was a compliment.

KERRY. He doesn't mean it.

FREYA. I get embarrassed by compliments.

KERRY. Pull the other one. You're not my teacher. I don't
know how we got going on this. It's all stupid.

*A slight pause.*

What?

*A slight pause.*

It's not my fault if I'm thick.

LEE. Tell her she's as bright as a button.

KERRY. You sound just like her. I'm not deaf. He's only
saying it because he wants to fuck me rigid.

LEE. Yer know something, Kerry. I can't do it properly. Last
time I tried, anyhow. Taking miles of heroin does that.

KERRY. Oh. Yer neither use nor ornament then, are yer.

*A slight pause.*

Yer let him take it. I don't know how you could. Yer meant to be helping him.

FREYA. Yes. He knows what I think.

KERRY. It don't do no good, far as I can see. Yer'll be saying he's a good lad next.

FREYA. No.

LEE. I am, aren't I?

FREYA. You're better, Lee, much better. But you're not perfect. You know that.

LEE. Thanks a bunch, Freya. I didn't think I was.

KERRY. What are you getting at him for?

FREYA. I'm not.

KERRY. You are. You don't know what yer doing half the time.

FREYA. I'm not getting at anyone, Kerry.

KERRY. Pull the other one.

*A slight pause.*

FREYA. Well, I should go.

FREYA *picks up the holdall.*

KERRY. Tell her she can't.

LEE. How? It's a free country.

KERRY. It isn't. Where d'you live – whatever yer name is – Freya.

FREYA. In Seamer.

LEE. It's a village over there.

KERRY. I know. I don't actually. What? It's not my fault. Whole place is rubbish. At least in Dormanstown yer know where you are.

FREYA. Is that where you go to school?

KERRY. It could be, it mightn't be. If you're so wise, you should tell us.

FREYA. Well, I'm going to be late.

KERRY. Yer like everyone else.

FREYA. Am I?

KERRY. I've just said so.

FREYA. Why?

KERRY. Yer not actually. I don't go in much for poshies. Are you his surrogate mam or something?

FREYA. Lee knows.

KERRY. You shouldn't be rude.

FREYA. I've an excellent teacher.

KERRY. What's that about? Yeh. I asked for it.

FREYA. You did.

KERRY. I don't mean none of it. I mean some of it. I don't know.

FREYA *puts the holdall in her other hand.*

Yer could give us some of them flowers.

FREYA *takes a flower from the bunch and gives it to her.* KERRY *smells it. She pulls off the petals one by one.*

So what, it was mine. Yer could give us another one if yer dare.

FREYA *gives her a flower.* KERRY *starts to pull off the petals.* FREYA *grabs her hand and stops her.*

That's abuse yer know.

FREYA. What?

KERRY. You touching us. Yer can be done for it.

KERRY *walks away. She bends down and plants the flower in the barley. The red petals poke out above the mist. She goes back to* FREYA, *and helps herself to another flower. She plants that in a similar way.*

Can I ask you a big favour?

FREYA. Yes.

KERRY. It's the biggest favour anyone's ever asked yer. Yer won't like it.

FREYA. Ask me.

KERRY. I don't like where I live. It's the bloody pox. It's fuckin' crap, it's fuckin' shit, I fuckin' hate it. Can I come and live with you?

*A slight pause.*

FREYA. I don't know.

KERRY *walks off. She goes.*

*There is a short silence.*

LEE. Our Ewan's gone and killed someone, Freya. He really has.

FREYA *looks down.*

Are you all right?

FREYA. No, I'm not all right, Lee.

DOMINIC *enters on a new bicycle. He is twenty one years old but looks slightly younger than that. He has a fresh face and wire-framed glasses. He is wearing jeans and a jumper. He comes to a halt and takes a carrier bag off the handle bars.*

DOMINIC. You forgot your tests, Mum. Who was that girl just now?

FREYA. She's a friend of Lee's.

DOMINIC. Is she your girlfriend, Lee?

LEE. I'm hopeful, Dom.

DOMINIC. D'you like my new bike?

LEE. It's very smart.

DOMINIC. It's brill. Mum and dad bought me it on Saturday morning. You can have a turn if you would like to. It's free by the way.

LEE. I'll have a go some other time.

FREYA. If they were on the dining room table, Dominic –

DOMINIC. Yes.

FREYA. I haven't finished marking them. I need them for tomorrow.

DOMINIC. Oh deary dear, my mistake. I think I'm going to catch her up and have a chat with her.

FREYA. No.

DOMINIC. Why not, Mum?

FREYA. For one thing it's rather misty and dangerous. For another thing she's Lee's girlfriend.

DOMINIC. Now you are being silly. He doesn't mind, do you?

LEE. You'd better do as your mum says, Dom.

DOMINIC. By the way, Lee, there's been a murder. It's on the radio news. Have you heard it?

LEE. Yes.

FREYA. Take them back and put them back on the table please, where you found them.

DOMINIC. Mum.

FREYA. Now, and no argument.

DOMINIC. Oh, you're so useless.

DOMINIC *turns the bike round and cycles off.*

FREYA. Well, why did you tell me?

LEE *shrugs.*

LEE. I'm a bit like a kid, I always tell you everything. Sorry. I should have more guile.

FREYA *walks somewhere.*

You're not going like?

FREYA. Where to, Lee? I'm not going anywhere for a minute.

LEE. Have I put you in a pickle? I have as well. It's a bit of an understatement.

FREYA. I ought to be getting used to it, but I'm not.

LEE. You know they'll come for us. They're bound to. I've had it.

FREYA. Were you there?

LEE. No. I promise you.

FREYA. Was it Ewan on his own?

LEE. Yeh.

FREYA. That's something I suppose. For pities sake, Lee, it's not much of a comfort when someone is dead. I don't know how you can.

LEE. It's not my fault. I didn't do it.

FREYA. It never is your fault.

LEE. It isn't.

FREYA. I know.

LEE. You don't know. I had nothing to do with it.

FREYA. Promise absolutely.

LEE. Yeh. I didn't.

FREYA. Why don't I believe you?

LEE. I don't know. I didn't.

*A slight pause.*

FREYA. You are in a mess.

LEE. It's obvious.

FREYA. You were in a mess before. You are always in a mess. When is it going to change?

*A slight pause.*

LEE. I wasn't going to tell you. It kind of slipped out. I'm sorry, Freya.

FREYA. I am sick of hearing you say sorry. I've heard it before. It has become completely meaningless. Don't you see that?

LEE. No.

FREYA. You haven't tried at all. You promised me.

LEE. I've tried more than you know as a matter-of-fact.

FREYA. I don't see the results, Lee. I see chaos.

*A slight pause.*

LEE. I see the results.

FREYA. Where?

LEE. In me. In us. You don't know how much I need you about like. In case yer think that's daft, it's only me being sort of honest. I mean I couldn't have said it if it hadn't have been for you.

FREYA. I know how much you need me, Lee. It's why it's so difficult sometimes.

LEE. I'm doing my best to show you the results as matter-of-fact.

LEE*'s knee starts to twitch.*

FREYA. You don't need another hit for goodness sake?

LEE. No.

LEE *wets himself.*

I've gone and pissed myself. I'm in a mess, Freya. This time I'm in a mess. I'm dead. I won't survive if they take me in. I'm not going through it again.

FREYA *goes to him.*

FREYA. What d'you mean?

LEE. I'm not going through it again. It's the worst there is. You don't know. It's not worth it.

*A slight pause.*

FREYA. You're wet.

LEE. It doesn't matter.

FREYA. Of course it matters.

LEE. It doesn't.

FREYA *delves into the holdall and finds the bottom part of a tracksuit.*

FREYA. Take your things off and put these on.

LEE. You're all right.

FREYA. Put – them – on. I'll turn the other way if it embarrasses you.

LEE. No.

LEE *unfastens his jeans. He starts to take them off.*

FREYA. They're not going to come off with your shoes still on. Don't be a halfpenny.

FREYA *kneels.*

LEE. You can't see properly.

FREYA. I'll manage.

FREYA *takes off his shoes. She takes off his jeans from round his feet, and gets up.* LEE *takes off his pants.* FREYA *takes a tee shirt from the holdall.*

Wipe yourself with this.

LEE. Thanks.

LEE *drys himself.* FREYA *looks the other way, even though* LEE*'s jumper is long enough to make it unnecessary. She holds out the bottoms of the tracksuit.* LEE *puts them on together with his shoes.*

FREYA. Are you done?

LEE. Yeh.

FREYA *turns.*

What're you smiling for?

FREYA. I was thinking about when you came to the house, scrumping apples, all those years ago, and Joachim caught you.

LEE. What about it?

FREYA. He made you promise you wouldn't come back.

LEE. It's like everything, Freya. I mean not to do it, then I do it again.

FREYA. I wonder why?

LEE *shrugs.*

LEE. I start again before I've stopped.

FREYA. It must end. How often have I said that? Far too often, Lee. There has to be a beginning sooner or later. Why can't you make it sooner?

LEE. It gets the better of us. I stop, then I'm off again before I know it. I haven't hurt anyone for a long time, have I?

FREYA. I know.

LEE. I hurt me. I only do it to myself.

FREYA. You don't.

LEE. I do.

FREYA. No. You hurt me as well.

LEE. Oh. I wasn't counting you like.

FREYA. Why not?

LEE. I was counting you as a matter-of-fact. I don't think of you in that way. I think of you as something else.

FREYA. Well, I wish you wouldn't. I'm someone who gets hurt.

LEE. I didn't know like.

LEE *looks down. He kicks the mist.*

FREYA. You know now.

LEE. Yeh.

*He looks up.*

Yer in a get-at-me mood.

FREYA. I'm never in a get-at-you mood.

LEE. I used to get angry at yer, scream and shout, kick and punch. Any excuse to get you to hate us, to show you loved us a bit really. A lot as a matter-of-fact. I'd be dead if it wasn't for you. Yer still don't know what it's like, Freya. I live on the edge. I don't even know on the edge of what. I love you, kind of thing.

FREYA. I know.

LEE. I spend most of my bloody time trying not to let you down. You're the only one who's ever cared about us. You say I should be weak. How weak is that? Is that weak enough for yer?

FREYA. Nearly.

LEE. Fuck you, Freya.

FREYA. Don't – you – ever – swear – at – me. Is that clear?

LEE. Fuck off. You fuckin' cunt.

LEE *walks off.*

FREYA. I would walk away if I was you, Lee.

LEE *turns. He points a finger.*

LEE. I'll fucking get you for this. I was being fuckin' honest with you.

FREYA. When honesty is enough I'll let you know.

LEE. Fuck. Fuck you.

FREYA. No, that isn't the right thing to say. Come on, come up with something else.

LEE. What?

FREYA. I'm waiting.

LEE. What? Tell us.

FREYA. You tell me.

LEE. I don't know what it is.

FREYA. I don't either. It's something though.

LEE. How am I suppose to know if you don't?

FREYA. Use your intelligence.

LEE. I haven't got any.

FREYA. Oh, well, if all you're going to do is feel sorry for yourself, we might as well go home.

LEE *thinks.*

LEE. I don't feel sorry for myself. Do I?

FREYA. Yes. All the time. You enjoy it. It makes you very happy. Very content.

LEE. I don't think so.

FREYA. Yes. You absolutely adore being a victim. You like nothing better than a good old bleat about how badly you're treated.

LEE. I don't.

FREYA. Yes, you do. It's why you enjoy victimising other people, Lee. You used to. There was a time. You're a victim, so why not make a few more. It's still there inside you.

LEE. I'm not a victim.

FREYA. Yes, you are.

*A slight pause.*

I've not hurt you.

LEE. You have as matter-of-fact. A bit.

FREYA. Have I? I thought you were impossible to hurt.

LEE. No.

*A slight pause.*

FREYA. I'm still waiting. As Ewan would say, I've got the patience of Job.

KERRY *comes on. She looks at* FREYA.

KERRY. I mean it you know.

*The Interval.*

## ACT TWO

### Scene One

*The garden at the house in Seamer. That night.*

*The garden is surrounded by a high, crumbling brick wall. There is a century-old, knurled apple tree. Above it is a full moon, so clear that it is possible to see the details of mountains and valleys. It is one of those nights when the moon appears to be unnaturally large.*

FREYA *is by the tree. She is wearing a whitish robe.*

JOACHIM SOERENSEN *enters. He is a hundred years old or thereabouts, a large man with a big face and hands, and unkempt blond hair. He was born in Denmark and still speaks with an accent. He is blind. He is wearing white trousers beneath a white dressing gown. He calls, not knowing if he will get a reply.*

JOACHIM. Freya.

    FREYA *turns and comes out of the shadow of the tree.*

FREYA. I'm here, Joachim.

JOACHIM. Why did I know you'd be out by the tree.

    JOACHIM *joins her.*

FREYA. It's my secret place, Papa dear.

    FREYA *kisses his forehead.*

JOACHIM. When you're fretting I get disturbed, and I can't sleep with the heat as it is.

FREYA. Well, I did wrong today.

JOACHIM. How long can I expect it to last? What did you do?

FREYA. I was angry with Lee when I shouldn't have been. He deserves better.

JOACHIM. You were always a fool to deal with those nobody people.

FREYA. Perhaps.

JOACHIM. I will not begin something unless I know how it ends.

FREYA. You're not yourself tonight.

JOACHIM. His nature is to be bad, as yours is to be good.

FREYA. Maybe.

JOACHIM. I get upset when I can make a difference.

FREYA. We're all different, Papa.

JOACHIM. You are in love with the child.

FREYA *kisses* JOACHIM*'s forehead.*

FREYA. Nonsense. You're dreaming.

JOACHIM. I would have contact with the boy if it would give me pleasure.

FREYA. I know, but it would be wrong.

JOACHIM. If you find yourself attracted to his nasty habits, why not. Violence is compelling to some.

FREYA. As you say often, Papa.

JOACHIM. Is it an untruth?

JOACHIM *brushes away some midges that are around his face.*

If I was you I would have sex so I could move on to another place.

FREYA. Perhaps. You're enjoying your own dreams as you always do.

JOACHIM. The midges are everywhere this summer.

FREYA *brushes away some midges for him.*

FREYA. And his brother has gone and killed someone, Papa. The murder in Stokesley. It was Ewan who hit the man so hard he died.

JOACHIM *swipes his hand in front of his face.*

JOACHIM. The flies. Who told you?

FREYA. Lee blurted it out in an unguarded moment.

JOACHIM. When a nobody tries to be somebody there is certain to be turmoil. You see what comes of meddling in English affairs.

FREYA. I can't unlearn what I know.

JOACHIM. It is not our concern, my love. It is Lee's responsibility.

FREYA. He'll do nothing, Papa. Anything he does is bound to put his brother in prison. What would you do in those circumstances?

JOACHIM. I would live with my conscience as he will have to. They are of no consequence these people. They have such low self-esteem. They do not believe any other human being is of any worth or merit at all.

FREYA *runs her fingers down* JOACHIM*'s arm.*

FREYA. I know, Papa. Please don't be grumpy.

JOACHIM *swipes away some midges.*

The fact is, I know what happened. Don't I have the same responsibility as Lee?

JOACHIM. You might if he had a value system. He does not have such a thing.

FREYA. You're wrong, Papa.

JOACHIM. I will not have the police come here to interrupt our lives.

FREYA. I know.

JOACHIM. I want none of their authority about this house.

FREYA. I feel the same, my darling. You're worrying over nothing.

FREYA *kisses* JOACHIM*'s lips.*

DOMINIC *enters. His hair is ruffled. He is wearing a baggy tee shirt and boxer shorts, which he sleeps in.*

DOMINIC. Dad, what's going on?

JOACHIM *turns.*

JOACHIM. Mum and me are talking, Dom.

FREYA. Go back to bed, Dominic. It's very late.

DOMINIC. I can't sleep anyway for thinking things over. It's time I was off your hands.

JOACHIM. What has brought this on?

DOMINIC. Only Lee. He has a girlfriend every time I meet him.

FREYA *goes towards him.*

FREYA. Come here, you daft halfpenny.

DOMINIC *joins her.* FREYA *ruffles his hair some more.*

It'll come. It'll happen.

DOMINIC. I wouldn't mind quite so much if I wasn't a virgin.

FREYA. Be patient.

DOMINIC. It hurts when I see everyone else, Mum. I don't think you quite realise. I'm a predicament to myself.

JOACHIM. I would go off and look for a whore, Dom, as I did do many times in my youth. It was my father's good advice, well proffered. He gave me the filthy lucre. Why? Because he was too busy with his mistress to be concerned with me. How old are you now?

DOMINIC. Twenty one.

JOACHIM. I was twelve or thirteen when I bedded my first whore, shyly as it was. I had a prick this size.

JOACHIM *holds up the end of his little finger.*

I knew a time when life was nothing without excess. No rational person, Dominic, has ever found themselves without first going to the limits.

DOMINIC. What's he on about, Mum?

FREYA. Goodness knows. He's about to get on his high horse. Either that or be silent for a week.

JOACHIM. Where are you, Dom?

DOMINIC. I'm by mum.

JOACHIM. I was twelve or thirteen in the Moulin Rouge in Paris, a girl swinging on each arm.

JOACHIM *thinks.*

DOMINIC. What about it, Dad?

FREYA. He's making it up. He's lost his thread.

JOACHIM. Yes, I have. It is all a little cloudy these days, my two loves. The facts and the fantasy have become the same, unfortunately for clear reason.

JOACHIM *delves into his trouser pocket and takes out a wodge of notes.*

I want my son to have a whore. How much is a whore these days? What are these?

FREYA *goes to him.*

FREYA. They're fifties, Joachim. Put them back.

JOACHIM *holds up five notes.* DOMINIC *takes them as his father puts the others away.*

DOMINIC. You're spoiling us, Dad.

JOACHIM. They are for a whore, and for whatever else it is you might want. Where are you?

DOMINIC. Here.

JOACHIM *runs his fingers about his son's face.*

JOACHIM. Let hedonism triumph for once.

JOACHIM *kisses* DOMINIC's *forehead.*

KERRY *enters. She is wearing jeans and a shirt which is not tucked in. She has a suitcase.*

KERRY. I've come, you know. I wasn't having you on or anything.

DOMINIC. It's that girl, Mum.

FREYA. Kerry.

JOACHIM. Who is it?

FREYA. It's Lee's girlfriend, Joachim.

FREYA *goes towards her.*

KERRY. I wouldn't be his girlfriend for all the tea in China.

JOACHIM. What time does the girl think it is?

KERRY. Don't you treat me like I'm daft.

KERRY *puts down the case.*

JOACHIM. What is she doing?

KERRY. Can't yer see or are you more of an idiot?

FREYA. He's blind, Kerry.

KERRY. Oh. Sorry. I'll know in future.

KERRY *is shy and looks at* DOMINIC.

DOMINIC. Well, I'm Dominic as matter-of-fact.

KERRY. It's what Lee says over and over, as a matter-of-fact.
He must have got it off you.

FREYA. It's the other way about.

KERRY. Is this the tree where Lee came pinching apples?

DOMINIC. I think so.

KERRY. He's told us about when he was a small lad. All about
how yer mum used to give him the apples in a bag like it
was a shop. He said you played shops. Did you?

DOMINIC. He was the shopkeeper and I was the customer,
except I didn't have any money because he always kept it. I
didn't mind.

KERRY. He said yer slow and that.

DOMINIC. I am, but I'm not sub-normal or even anything
bordering on it. Am I, Mum?

FREYA. No.

KERRY. Yer a pin-up in yer boxer shorts. Dead sexy.

DOMINIC. I'm not. Thanks. I'll take them off.

FREYA. No, Dominic.

DOMINIC *stops. He pulls them back up.*

KERRY. Yer two thirds of a full loaf. I said you look sexy with
them on.

DOMINIC. I wish you'd make up your mind.

FREYA. Joachim.

JOACHIM. Yes.

FREYA. I'm going to run Kerry home.

JOACHIM. Very good.

>   KERRY *sits on the case.*

FREYA. Come on. Your mum will be worrying.

KERRY. It's obvious yer don't know me mam.

>   KERRY *rubs her knee.*

>   I bruised me knee climbing over the wall for a start off.

>   JOACHIM *takes a fifty pound note from his pocket and goes towards her.*

JOACHIM. Here.

>   KERRY *hesitates.*

FREYA. Take it.

KERRY. Thanks like.

>   KERRY *takes the money.*

>   LEE *enters. He is wearing jeans and a tee shirt.*

JOACHIM. Who's there?

FREYA. It's Lee.

DOMINIC. Now then, Lee.

LEE. Now then, kidda.

DOMINIC. Is she your girlfriend, Lee?

LEE. I don't know, Dom.

>   JOACHIM *takes a fifty pound note from his pocket.*

JOACHIM. Lee. Where are you?

LEE. No thanks.

JOACHIM. Take it.

LEE. No. I won't.

>   *The church clock a few hundred yards away begins to chime midnight.*

>   HAZEL *enters. She is wearing a skirt.*

>   She followed us, Kerry.

HAZEL. Yer give yer kids more of everything and all they do is let you down. Don't think yer stealing her like yer tried to put sense into him. Yer won't. You and yer imbecile lad. He took his trousers down in the woods, didn't he once? I know the gossip about yer. Are you his dad or his granddad? Yer the muck on the street.

JOACHIM *takes the wodge of notes from his pocket and offers her quite a few.*

JOACHIM. Here.

HAZEL. Don't you care who I am?

JOACHIM. No.

HAZEL. I'm her mother.

JOACHIM. Take it.

HAZEL. I'll take it all right.

HAZEL *takes the money.*

KERRY. I'm not coming, Mam.

JOACHIM. You people.

HAZEL. What about us people?

JOACHIM. You are junk.

HAZEL. Is that it?

JOACHIM. Yes.

HAZEL. We look after our own. You remember it when yer get sick of their lardy ways.

KERRY. I'll come and see you and that.

HAZEL. Yer will, will yer?

KERRY. Yeh.

HAZEL. I might not be in.

JOACHIM. Lee we know. Will you take your unpleasant family and go away.

HAZEL. I am in my own good time. Is she your daughter or is she your wife? Kerry, we're going.

HAZEL *grabs* KERRY*'s arm.*

KERRY. Get off us. I'm not.

HAZEL. Get up.

KERRY. No.

FREYA. Stop it.

DOMINIC. What's going on, Mum?

FREYA. Nothing. Nothing.

LEE. It's all right, Dom.

DOMINIC. Do you know what's going on, Lee?

LEE. Yer mum's right.

HAZEL. Get yersell up.

KERRY. It's not gone in, has it, Mam. I'm staying put.

FREYA. Joachim, she can stay with us tonight.

KERRY. You don't know what she's like.

FREYA. I do. Joachim?

JOACHIM. Yes.

KERRY. You won't regret it. Thanks, Mister.

HAZEL. I'll tell the police on yer.

JOACHIM. You abuse and you accuse, whoever you are. You do so much with so little. Where are you, Lee?

LEE. Here.

JOACHIM. Take her away before I lose my temper.

LEE. The door's locked.

JOACHIM. You know where the key is.

LEE. Yeh.

LEE *goes to the tree. He takes an old iron key off a nail.*

HAZEL. Yer won't get away with it. I'll think of something. I've not got a screw loose.

JOACHIM. So far you have proved yourself to be incapable of thought. I doubt it will change.

HAZEL. I'll be back.

JOACHIM. No.

HAZEL *goes off with* LEE.

*There is a short silence.*

FREYA. Joachim.

JOACHIM. Where is she?

FREYA. Here. Joachim, there was nothing else I could do.

JOACHIM. I know.

JOACHIM *has joined them.*

FREYA. She's sitting.

FREYA *takes* KERRY*'s arm.*

KERRY. What?

KERRY *stands up.* JOACHIM *feels around her face with the ends of his fingers.* KERRY *flinches.*

JOACHIM. I am not going to hurt you.

KERRY. It's tickly.

JOACHIM. Of course it is. There are a few rules if you are to stay here.

KERRY. What like?

JOACHIM. You must be civilised. You must be polite. Already I have heard you shout too much. There are virtues in being private. You are too public.

KERRY. Oh.

JOACHIM *searches her face vigorously, using his palms.*

You're hurting us.

JOACHIM. I make the rules. Do you understand?

KERRY. Yeh.

JOACHIM *stops.*

JOACHIM. You are a pretty girl.

KERRY. I'm not.

JOACHIM. Who is going to think you pretty if you don't?

KERRY. You just did.

JOACHIM. Touché.

KERRY. Did I do that right?

JOACHIM. Yes.

KERRY. A bit of luck.

JOACHIM. Who is going to know you are ingenious if you don't?

*A slight pause.*

Well?

KERRY. I'm thinking about it.

JOACHIM. Who is going to know you think when you very rarely do?

KERRY. Is these some of the rules? If they are I'm getting lost.

JOACHIM. Yes.

KERRY. Funny rules. They're dead easy actually. I thought yer meant don't do this, don't do that.

JOACHIM. No.

KERRY. Oh. I'm going to have a brilliant time.

FREYA. Joachim.

JOACHIM. Yes.

KERRY. Are you foreign and that? Daft question.

JOACHIM. Yes.

KERRY. I was really asking yer where yer from?

JOACHIM. I was born in Prague.

FREYA. Kerry.

KERRY. Hold on please.

JOACHIM. My mother was Danish, from Århus in Jutland, and my father was Czech. He smuggled diamonds. He was a criminal and a very excellent one. My mother was a dancer who was photographed throughout Europe. The jewels went in her portmanteaux, from country to country.

FREYA. Joachim.

JOACHIM. Be quiet. Is your mother as good as her word?

KERRY. What?

JOACHIM. Will she go to the Stokesley police?

KERRY. Me mam? She won't let them in the house over Dennis the menace. She hates them more than me. She killed our Ryan when he was a baby. She was only fourteen. She's been in homes and done time herself. She was put away.

FREYA *goes to* JOACHIM *and takes hold of his hand.*

FREYA. It's only me.

JOACHIM *feels his wrist watch.*

JOACHIM. It's after midnight. Where's Lee?

FREYA. You sent him off. It's bedtime.

DOMINIC. I'm not an imbecile. Am I, Mum?

FREYA. No, of course not.

JOACHIM. Where has the girl gone to?

FREYA. She's here.

JOACHIM. Is there anything that affects and touches you? Very good.

JOACHIM *walks towards the house.* FREYA *goes with him. They go.*

*A slight pause.*

KERRY. Do yer mam and dad sleep in different rooms and that?

DOMINIC. Yes.

KERRY. Yer dead lucky you are.

DOMINIC. I don't need you to tell me.

KERRY. Can I ask you something? Is Lee all right?

DOMINIC. What do you mean?

KERRY. Is he good fun and that?

DOMINIC. He's my oldest friend.

KERRY. Yeh. Is he reliable and stuff?

DOMINIC. Yes.

*A slight pause.*

KERRY. Yer mum and dad are something else.

DOMINIC. I know.

KERRY. Yer dead nice.

DOMINIC. Will you be my girlfriend?

KERRY *smiles and thinks.*

KERRY. No.

DOMINIC. Sorry.

KERRY. It's one of the best offers I've ever had.

DOMINIC. Why?

KERRY. Yer too lovely.

DOMINIC. I'm not. I'm quite bad as matter-of-fact.

KERRY. If you're bad then there's no hope for any of us.

DOMINIC. What do you mean?

KERRY. I'm dead envious.

DOMINIC. I'm envious of you as matter-of-fact. I think you're lovely.

KERRY. You don't.

DOMINIC. I know what I think.

KERRY. I'm not lovely, Dominic.

DOMINIC. You are to me.

KERRY. If I went out with you, I'd only let you down.

DOMINIC. You wouldn't.

KERRY. I'm a lot like Lee. I can't help myself. I mean to stop meself doing stuff, then I do it again.

DOMINIC. You're your own worst enemy.

KERRY. Is that what Lee says he is?

DOMINIC. Yes.

KERRY. Yer brilliant. What's brilliant is yer don't know it. I'm a cow.

DOMINIC. If you think you're a cow what is everyone else supposed to think?

KERRY. Yer copying yer dad. Yer worth more.

DOMINIC. I'm not copying my father.

KERRY. Oh.

DOMINIC. I thought that up myself.

    FREYA *enters.*

KERRY. Is it true what he said?

FREYA. Who, Kerry? What?

KERRY. About the jewels and stuff?

FREYA. No. He gets muddled. I'll take you in.

KERRY. Can I ask you some stuff?

FREYA. About what?

KERRY. You and him and that.

FREYA. No. Not now. It's far too late.

KERRY. D'you love him?

FREYA. Yes, very much.

KERRY. I bet you he's as bossy as hell.

FREYA. He can be.

KERRY. I know you love him. It's as obvious as the nose on your face. Like I said to Dominic, I don't love anyone.

FREYA. You will.

KERRY. Will I?

FREYA. I'm sure.

KERRY. I love me dad a bit, as a matter-of-fact.

    FREYA *goes to the case.*

FREYA. I'll take you in.

KERRY. I love him a lot.

FREYA. Do you?

KERRY. Yeh.

FREYA. I'll take you in.

**Scene Two**

*A pig field. The following afternoon.*

*There is a pig hut which is made out of an upturned semi-circle of corrugated tin. It is enclosed by wood at the back and is half open at the front. The sun is strong, flattening out the light and making the tin shimmer*

KERRY *is there.*

EWAN *comes out of the pig hut. He has a clear plastic bag with lots of small, tin foil sachets in it. He takes off his tee shirt, spreads it on the grass and tips out the sachets onto it. He begins to count them.*

KERRY. You shouldn't do that.

EWAN. Have yer got it in mind to be Pope? Pope Pious?

KERRY. No. You kill people you do.

EWAN. People don't need me to kill themselves. Kerry, Kerry.

KERRY. Yer about as sexy as half a slice of bread with no butter.

    LEE *enters.*

LEE. What yer doing?

KERRY. I only saw him, honest I did. I was coming looking for yer.

EWAN. It's Dormanstown day, Lee. Shouldn't you be at school?

KERRY. Yes. I've done all me exams. I won't pass so what's the point?

EWAN. Where've yer been all day, our kid?

LEE. The police have had me in like.

EWAN. There'd be more evidence in the tea leaves in the canteen.

LEE. I know. They know it, too. They've got Dean in again an' all.

EWAN. The ridiculous ponce'll go and confess, you wait and see if I'm not right.

EWAN *goes into the hut*

KERRY. I'm not even partly with him.

LEE. Aren't you? Are you sure?

KERRY. Yeh.

*A pair of jeans and shoes come flying out of the hut.* EWAN *follows them out.*

EWAN. Tell us what that is if it's not evidence.

LEE *wanders away.* KERRY *looks at the blood-stained clothes.*

KERRY. Yer completely disgusting you are.

EWAN. You love it.

KERRY. You couldn't be more wrong. I don't know how you can.

EWAN. What?

KERRY. Be as you are.

EWAN. He was scum.

KERRY. That's a good one coming from you.

EWAN. Are you off, Lee?

LEE *turns and shakes his head.*

LEE. I've got a headache.

EWAN *picks up the tee shirt and puts it on top of the hut.*

EWAN. What did they say to yer?

LEE. The usual guff.

KERRY. Did they ask yer about him?

LEE. Yeh.

EWAN *picks up a couple of sachets.*

EWAN. It's Christmas in July.

LEE *goes to him and takes them.* KERRY *wanders off.* EWAN *counts the sachets.*

LEE. I had to tell them a few things or I'd be in there next week.

EWAN. What about, kid?

LEE. I had to admit to some burglaries. I needed to toot.
They've got me by the scruff of the neck, our lad. They told
us which I'd done and I went along with it.

KERRY *goes to* LEE.

KERRY. Let's have a look at yer arm.

LEE. I do it in me ankle, Kerry. I've got to get me smack to
feel normal again. Don't they know it an' all.

KERRY. Have they charged you?

LEE. Yeh. I'm in court tomorrow.

LEE *goes inside the hut.* EWAN *plays with one of his
nipples.*

EWAN. Yer love it.

KERRY. You'd go to your own funeral and still not care much.

EWAN. I'm a wholesaler. Kerry, Kerry. I don't use. Come and
live at me mam's. I promise.

KERRY. You chuck promises around. You know your trouble?

EWAN. Tell us.

KERRY. Yer'll never change, is your trouble.

EWAN *grabs hold of her arm.*

EWAN. Yer hardly grateful, considering.

KERRY. Considering what?

EWAN. You tell me, Joan of Arc.

KERRY. What's that about, if yer know?

EWAN. She was a martyr.

KERRY. I don't even like you.

EWAN. Yer thrive on it.

LEE. Dig dig dig dig diig.

EWAN. Admit it.

KERRY. What?

EWAN. You revel in it. You're hooked on me.

KERRY. Who'd want to have your kids?

EWAN. You do.

KERRY. There's plenty enough of you, without making any
more.

LEE. Dig dig dig dig diig.

EWAN. I'd be your guardian angel, Kerry.

KERRY. You wouldn't.

EWAN. Yeh, I would.

KERRY. No.

EWAN. Oh yeh.

*KERRY kisses him. They kiss.*

*The clock in the town half a mile away begins to chime four
o'clock.*

*DOMINIC enters riding his bike. He is going fast. He
comes to a halt.*

DOMINIC. Excuse me. What are you kissing him for?

KERRY. I wasn't.

EWAN. It's little Hard-on.

DOMINIC. Where's Lee by the way?

*LEE comes out of the hut.*

I'm on a world record attempt as a matter-of-fact. You can
have a turn if you would like to.

*LEE leans against the hut.*

Are you all right, Lee?

LEE. Yeh.

DOMINIC. I go round the town. I go right round Stokesley in
under eighteen minutes.

EWAN. How's yer mam these days, Hard-on?

DOMINIC. She's very well, thank you for asking.

*EWAN goes to DOMINIC.*

EWAN. It's a grand machine.

KERRY. Leave him be, Ewan.

EWAN. Is yer dad still giving her one now and again, old as he is? Is he still dusting it off?

LEE. Dig dig dig dig diig.

EWAN. He's old enough to be your granddad, isn't he?

DOMINIC *gets off the bike.*

DOMINIC. I didn't mean you could have a turn. I meant Lee.

KERRY. I'm sitting on it, so there.

KERRY *sits on the bike.*

EWAN. I thought you'd be at work, Hard-on.

DOMINIC. It's my day off.

EWAN. Yer a fetch-this fetch-that at Sainsbury's Homebase, aren't yer?

DOMINIC. I don't think it's any of your business.

KERRY. It's a better job than yours any day of the month.

EWAN. Yer addicted to us, Miss Florence Nightingale.

KERRY. Yeh, I want to be a nurse. I'm going to look after old people.

DOMINIC. Are you his girlfriend, Kerry?

KERRY. No.

DOMINIC. We're two peas in a pod.

EWAN. We're not.

KERRY. Yer know something? Yer a real coward, you are.

EWAN. Have I touched him? Have I hurt him? I could do. It's no pleasure.

DOMINIC *looks at the clothes.*

DOMINIC. Whose are those? Has someone been in a fight?

EWAN. Yeh.

DOMINIC. You, Ewan?

EWAN. Yeh. For her.

KERRY. Yer daft.

EWAN. I must be.

KERRY. Yer make me laugh.

EWAN. I fuckin' adore you.

DOMINIC. I do as well.

EWAN. I almost feel fuckin' ashamed of meself because of you.

KERRY. Yer sad. Yer pathetic.

DOMINIC. Me?

KERRY. Him. You want yer ball back all the time, don't yer.

LEE. Kerry.

KERRY. What?

LEE. Give it a rest for a bit please.

KERRY. I won't. When are you going to stick up for us any road?

LEE. I will when you do.

EWAN. She gets her rocks off on it.

KERRY. Yeh, I do.

EWAN. She's mental for us.

DOMINIC. What are you talking about?

EWAN. We're talking about yer dad and yer granddad.

LEE. Leave him alone, Ewan. He's done nothing to you.

EWAN. You catch on quick, kid. You should have been awake two minutes ago. You and your little friend always making things sweet.

*FREYA enters. She is carrying the holdall.*

DOMINIC. Mum.

FREYA. Hello.

EWAN. Oh yeh, I remember, you and her. I would watch her take care of you. Yeh, I was jealous. Covetous. D'you think I'd hurt him? No. I love you too much, our lad.

*He looks at KERRY.*

I delivered him. Oh yeh I did. When me mam's waters broke and she was in the kitchen. I caught hold of him as he popped out. I was the first person to wrap him up. Oh yeh. Me mam was so drunk she'd gone to sleep. I'll get you. Kerry, Kerry.

KERRY. No, yer won't.

EWAN. I will.

KERRY. No.

EWAN. I'm always successful.

KERRY. Yer won't.

FREYA. You were always welcome, Ewan.

EWAN. You didn't like me. I don't go where I'm not wanted. Never did.

*EWAN goes to the hut. He kisses LEE on the forehead.*

Yer gave him things. Yer didn't give me anything. Nothing. Why?

FREYA. You didn't ask me to.

EWAN. No. I was too fucking polite.

*EWAN wraps up the sachets in the tee shirt. He looks at the clothes.*

I'll leave them for the pigs.

*EWAN starts to go. FREYA stops him.*

FREYA. Wait.

EWAN. Get off us. I love her, Freya. There was a time I might have loved you, me mam was so useless. You were everything in the world to me. She's gone and got the better of us, like you did. I don't know why.

FREYA. Go to the police and tell them the truth.

EWAN. Yer must think I'm a bigger idiot than I do.

FREYA. I'll come with you.

EWAN. Like yer went with him?

FREYA. Yes.

EWAN. He did time. See him now. I don't see much you could say was glorious. He's a bigger mess than me if that's possible. Very sorry, my sweet.

FREYA. Please.

EWAN. No. Go screw yourself, or let yer dad fuck yer.

*EWAN goes.*

DOMINIC. Did he do the murder in Stokesley? I think he did by the way.

FREYA. Please don't ask.

DOMINIC. What's more I expect to know, Mum.

FREYA. Yes.

DOMINIC. Yes he did it, or yes what?

FREYA. Yes, he did it. Didn't he, Lee?

LEE. Yes.

FREYA. Didn't he, Kerry?

KERRY. Yes.

DOMINIC. Blimey. Now what?

*KERRY gets off the bike. FREYA goes to DOMINIC and runs her hand down the top of his arm.*

FREYA. Listen to me. It's a special secret like you.

LEE. D'you remember all those secrets when we were kids, Dom?

*DOMINIC takes the fifty pound notes from his pocket.*

DOMINIC. I don't mind paying you one little bit.

KERRY. Is he on about what I think he's on about?

FREYA. Dominic, don't be silly.

DOMINIC. I'm going to have my own secret for a change. Is this about right?

KERRY. Yer more mad than bonkers.

FREYA. Put it away.

KERRY. I might take you up on it, Dom.

FREYA. Kerry.

KERRY. Yer rude twit. Yer silly thing.

DOMINIC. I was hoping to do it for nothing at one time. Isn't it enough?

KERRY. I've just said. Clean yer ears out. Yer too kind and likeable. How many times do I have to tell you?

KERRY *lets go of the bike.* DOMINIC *takes hold of it.*

DOMINIC. I don't want to be kind and likeable.

KERRY. I don't want to be as I am either. It's the way it is. Someone tell him.

KERRY *wanders to the pig hut.* FREYA *starts to bundle up the clothes.* LEE *goes to her.*

LEE. I'll get rid of them. I'll put them somewhere.

FREYA. Will you? They're your brother's, aren't they?

LEE. Yeh.

FREYA. They're quite horrid, Lee. Where?

LEE. I know. I'll think of somewhere.

FREYA *gets up.*

FREYA. Home.

DOMINIC. I'm staying out with my friends.

FREYA. I've had quite enough for one day, Dominic. I'm in no mood to argue with you.

FREYA *picks up the holdall. She goes.*

DOMINIC. Well, hasn't she had a bad day at school.

LEE. Go with yer mum, Dom.

DOMINIC. No. I'm not. Why should I?

LEE. She wants you to.

DOMINIC. I'm not going to do anything she wants from now on.

LEE. Don't be like that.

DOMINIC. I think you are. She likes you more than me sometimes.

LEE. She doesn't.

DOMINIC. She does, you'll be pleased to know.

*A slight pause.*

It's all right, I know when I'm not wanted. I know what a gooseberry is.

KERRY. Your mum loves you.

DOMINIC. Here, I mean. You and him.

LEE. Have you any fags, Dom?

DOMINIC. No, I've given up.

*A slight pause.*

KERRY. Go with yer mam. Yer making us feel guilty.

DOMINIC. She's always wandering off these days.

LEE *bundles up the clothes, wrapping the shoes in the jeans. He picks up the bundle and goes off.*

I'm far too mollycoddled.

KERRY. Yeh, I've seen.

DOMINIC. Where's he gone?

KERRY. Your guess is as good as mine.

DOMINIC. I've come to the conclusion there isn't such a thing as being grown-up.

KERRY. I don't know.

DOMINIC. Why not?

KERRY. I just don't.

*A slight pause.*

DOMINIC. I'm glad I'm me.

KERRY. I am as well.

DOMINIC. I'm shy.

KERRY. Yeh.

DOMINIC. D'you like my bike?

LEE *comes back without the clothes.*

Where did you go?

LEE. I went for a piss.

DOMINIC. Oh.

KERRY. What are those secrets you said about?

LEE. I didn't say about any secrets.

KERRY. You did.

LEE. It isn't anything.

KERRY. I know anyway, so there.

DOMINIC. Lee used to stick up for me when I was bullied very badly at school.

LEE. Not at school, Dom. Here.

DOMINIC. Oh yes. My mistake.

LEE. Yer getting nearly as bad as yer dad.

LEE *takes off his tee shirt. He lies on the grass in the sun.* DOMINIC *puts his bike on the grass. He starts to unbutton and take off his shirt.*

KERRY. He's not getting undressed, is he?

LEE. Yer not getting undressed are you, Dom?

DOMINIC. No.

KERRY. I couldn't cope.

LEE. I thought you wanted to be a nurse?

KERRY. I do.

LEE. He did do once.

KERRY. I know.

LEE. He was dared so it hardly counts.

KERRY. Who?

LEE. Some little lasses.

KERRY. Serves them right.

DOMINIC *lies on the grass.* LEE *puts his tee shirt under his head.* DOMINIC *copies him and does the same thing with his shirt.* KERRY *sits on the grass near* LEE.

You know you said you was in court.

LEE. Yeh.

KERRY. Is it tomorrow?

LEE *leans his head on his elbow. He looks at* KERRY *and talks quietly.*

LEE. I don't talk about it in front of him. He doesn't always get it but he sometimes does.

KERRY. Some burglaries and that?

LEE. I think I did one of them. I can't remember.

KERRY. Have you told Freya?

LEE. You heard me. I didn't.

KERRY. I'll tell her. She'll sort it out.

LEE. I'll go down for absolute definite. I needed a hit. Short-term heaven, long-term hell.

KERRY. Yeh.

DOMINIC. What are you talking about?

LEE. Nothing, Dom.

*A slight pause.*

KERRY. You know the gossip and that.

LEE. What?

KERRY. About him and them. Is it true?

LEE. Yeh.

KERRY. How long have yer known?

LEE. Ages.

KERRY. It's a bit disgusting really.

LEE. Yer'd better not say owt.

KERRY. I won't. I daren't. Joachim – what's his name – he scares me.

LEE. He's a sculptor.

KERRY. He's a what?

LEE. Your dad's famous, isn't he?

DOMINIC. Yes.

KERRY. Do they still – you know?

LEE. No.

KERRY. Did Freya tell you?

LEE. Yeh.

*A slight pause.*

KERRY. I don't half like you, Lee.

LEE. I like you. I'll be going inside though.

KERRY. Yer won't. It'll be all right, you'll see. I'll speak up for you in court and that. And Freya will. She's dead good. I'll say I'm having your baby or something. That'll do it.

LEE. Yer not and it won't.

KERRY. Yer sound like yer want to go in.

LEE. No. I'm all right at the minute. I'm a bit high.

DOMINIC *sits up.*

DOMINIC. Will you talk to me, please?

LEE. Sorry, Dom.

DOMINIC *gets up and sits down beside them.*

KERRY. Were you at school together?

LEE. He's older than me. He went to a private school. It was a kind of special school for special people.

DOMINIC. It wasn't really, as a matter-of-fact. It was an ordinary school for people like me. I'm not special by the way.

LEE. I know.

DOMINIC. Why did you say it then?

LEE. I was praising you.

DOMINIC. Oh.

LEE. Yer getting yer knickers in a twist.

KERRY. I'd get him if I was you, Dominic.

DOMINIC. What?

KERRY *starts to tickle* LEE. DOMINIC *joins in.* LEE *giggles.*

LEE. Get off us. Get off us, yer big bullies.

KERRY *stops.* DOMINIC *stops and lies back with his head on* LEE's *stomach.* KERRY *looks at them for a moment. She runs her fingers through* LEE's *hair.* LEE *turns and looks at her.* KERRY *stops.*

KERRY. Sorry.

LEE. Why?

KERRY. I don't know. I feel daft. Nothing this good has ever happened to me. I'm mixed-up dead bad. Yer know what I really want?

LEE. Yeh, I think I do.

KERRY. Yer don't. I want to be a nurse. I think you and him are really brilliant. I'm dead envious. He doesn't half trust you. It's my fault.

LEE. Yeh, it is.

KERRY. I don't know why I said it about Dennis the menace. It was whim. I will stand up in court, you know. D'you think we should tell the truth?

LEE *thinks for a moment.*

LEE. No.

KERRY. I don't mind. I'd rather.

LEE. You'd do time, Kerry.

KERRY. I'd rather do time and get it out the way. I wouldn't do much any road. I didn't do it.

LEE. I wouldn't.

KERRY. Wouldn't you?

LEE. No.

KERRY. It'd be better for you.

LEE. They'll do me anyway.

KERRY. You could say about Dom and that, how he needs you and stuff.

LEE. Freya wrote to the judge last time. It makes no difference. Yer living in cloud cuckoo land. You've got to live with what you've done, Kerry. There's no excuses. You should talk to Freya about it.

KERRY. Yeh.

LEE. She's great. She knows.

KERRY. There's consequences all the time, isn't there?

LEE. Yeh.

KERRY. Will you stop taking drugs for me please.

LEE. I've tried stopping for him.

DOMINIC. Do you take drugs, Lee?

LEE. Of course I don't, you silly sod.

DOMINIC. You smoke cigarettes.

LEE. That's different.

DOMINIC. You'd tell me if you did, wouldn't you?

LEE. Of course I would. We're best mates, aren't we?

DOMINIC. Yes.

LEE. Best mates look after each other, Dom, no matter what.


**Scene Three**

*The conservatory at the house in Seamer. Late the following afternoon.*

*The conservatory is built almost entirely of glass, with a pointed glass roof. It is pentagonal and spacious. There are many windows, some of which are open, and white Venetian blinds, some of which are pulled down but the room is still very light and airy. A grape vine is growing up one of the corners and across part of the roof. There are some soft chairs and a few bentwood chairs put to one side. There is an oak dining-table protected by a white sheet. On it is a wood and wire armature.*

DOMINIC *is sitting in his stockinged feet. He has his knees up with his head resting on them.*

JOACHIM *enters carrying a plastic bucket covered in a damp cloth. He is wearing a white suit. He goes to the table and puts the bucket on an old stool.*

DOMINIC. Dad, are you my granddad as well?

   JOACHIM *takes a lump of clay from the bucket and begins to built it up around the armature.*

JOACHIM. I thought it was you sitting there, come in from work and thinking about the world. I love you twice.

DOMINIC. Where's mum?

JOACHIM. She has taken the afternoon off school to go to court with Lee and Kerry.

DOMINIC. Is Lee in court? What for?

JOACHIM. Burglary, if I remember, and goodness knows what else.

JOACHIM *takes some more clay from the bucket.*

Our heads make a noise when we think.

DOMINIC. Mine does. It's a funny situation to be in.

JOACHIM. Is it? What is? We are alike. There is a real world somewhere, but it does not concern us. Let the rest of humankind be envious if they want to be.

DOMINIC. Are you famous?

JOACHIM. Who said?

DOMINIC. Lee said.

JOACHIM. I suppose so.

DOMINIC. What for?

JOACHIM. For my figures of young girls amongst other things.

DOMINIC. Is that all?

JOACHIM. If I had not been as I am, it would have been different. I am not supposed to see and touch enough to be erotic. I cannot look at a nude girl. Where are you?

DOMINIC. I'm still here.

JOACHIM. Very good.

DOMINIC. Can I see them?

JOACHIM. You have seen them, those that are left.

DOMINIC. Those?

JOACHIM. Yes. You see them day to day. What is the matter with you?

DOMINIC *takes off his socks. He sits with his head on his knees.* JOACHIM *is putting more clay on the armature.*

DOMINIC. I was thinking.

JOACHIM. What about?

DOMINIC. About me. It's so difficult.

JOACHIM. We think about ourselves all the time if we are gifted.

DOMINIC. I don't understand at all why you're my granddad as well as my dad.

JOACHIM. There is nothing very much to understand. Your mother and I love each other. Who said this to you?

DOMINIC. I trust Lee.

JOACHIM. I know.

DOMINIC. Should I trust him, Dad?

JOACHIM. Of course.

DOMINIC. Phew.

JOACHIM. Were you doubtful? You should not be.

DOMINIC *thinks.*

DOMINIC. I know a few things and then I think I don't. I get really fed up with it.

JOACHIM. Do you?

DOMINIC. Yes. Especially at the moment. I have a mind that doesn't work properly. Do I?

JOACHIM. We all do if we are sensible and creative.

FREYA *enters. She is wearing her best summer dress and shoes.*

Who is it, Dom?

DOMINIC. It's mum.

JOACHIM. Freya?

FREYA. I'm here.

FREYA *goes to him and kisses his forehead.*

JOACHIM. What happened?

FREYA. It was postponed until next month.

JOACHIM. Very good.

FREYA. He got bail. I've brought him home with me. He's going to stay with us for a few days.

JOACHIM. Very good.

FREYA. Are you sure, Joachim?

JOACHIM. Yes.

FREYA. I'm going to get some lemonade. I'm very hot.

FREYA *picks up the socks and goes out.*

DOMINIC. It was only mum.

JOACHIM. Yes, I know.

JOACHIM *slaps some clay on the armature.* DOMINIC *gets up and starts to go out.*

She is coming back.

DOMINIC. Oh.

DOMINIC *sits on the chair with his knees up. He takes a Gameboy from his pocket and plays it.* JOACHIM *stops what he is doing.*

JOACHIM. I never knew who my father was. Dom?

DOMINIC. Yes. What?

JOACHIM. Did you hear me?

DOMINIC. Yes.

JOACHIM. I always wanted you to know I was your father.

DOMINIC. I do.

KERRY *enters. She is wearing her best jeans and top.*

JOACHIM. Who is it?

DOMINIC. It's Kerry. Where's Lee?

KERRY. He's coming.

DOMINIC *plays the Gameboy.* JOACHIM *puts some clay on the armature.* KERRY *looks at the conservatory. She ends up at the table.*

Is that what you do?

JOACHIM. It's something of what I do.

KERRY. Lee told us he'd show us some art books you were in.

LEE *enters. He is wearing his best jeans and shirt.*

JOACHIM. Is that him?

KERRY. Yes.

DOMINIC. Do you want to go upstairs and play on the computer for an hour?

LEE. I'll have a go later on.

DOMINIC. Do you, Kerry?

KERRY. I'll come with you when he does.

FREYA *enters with a tray. On it is a glass jug full of lemonade, and five glasses. She puts it on the table.*

JOACHIM. Freya?

FREYA. Who else, my love?

DOMINIC *plays the Gameboy.* FREYA *pours the lemonade.*

DOMINIC. Mum, why is dad my granddad?

FREYA. We've visitors, Dominic.

DOMINIC. Lee's not a visitor.

FREYA. Kerry is a visitor.

FREYA *gives* KERRY *a glass of lemonade. She gives one to* LEE.

DOMINIC. Don't I get one?

FREYA *takes* DOMINIC *a glass of lemonade.*

FREYA. Don't be rude. You're not the centre of everyone's attention.

DOMINIC. I'm sorry for living. I won't in future.

FREYA. Enough is enough.

DOMINIC *hides his face in his knees.*

And don't get upset.

DOMINIC. I'll do what I like. They're my friends anyhow.

FREYA *goes back to the table. She puts a glass of lemonade into* JOACHIM*'s hand. He drinks.* DOMINIC *looks up.*

I don't have a very retentive memory, you know that. I'm very good at some things, but you forget the rest. This afternoon I couldn't remember where the cat litter and pet things were kept. I had to say I was sorry. The lady thought I was an idiot, which I'm not as matter-of-fact. I think quite deeply about things by the way. My head makes a noise. That's all. And I'm not upset.

DOMINIC *puts the glass of lemonade on the floor and plays the Gameboy.* KERRY *looks at* LEE. FREYA *goes to* DOMINIC.

Don't you dare be sympathetic by the way. I'm just not in the mood. I'm busy, thank you.

FREYA *takes the Gameboy off him.* DOMINIC *tries to grab it back.*

Give me it. It's mine.

FREYA. No.

DOMINIC. I hate you.

FREYA. You don't.

DOMINIC. I wish I was Lee with every bone in my body.

FREYA. Do you? He wishes he was you. Sometimes, not all the time. He might not say it, but there are odd moments when he does.

DOMINIC. Do you, Lee?

LEE. Yes.

FREYA. You might have told him. You have a responsibility.

LEE. I don't have any responsibility, Freya.

FREYA. I know. Don't I know. You take and you take and you take.

LEE. It's my life.

FREYA. It's not your life. No one's life is their's completely. You hurt people along the way. I was in that court this afternoon for you, and you've yet to thank me.

LEE. Thank you.

FREYA. Mean it.

LEE. I do. I love him. I did everything you wanted. You hurt, you really know how to hurt me.

LEE *starts to go.*

Come on, Dom, we'll play those computer games.

DOMINIC *gets up.*

FREYA. Go and you get out of this house.

LEE *stops.*

It's not perfect, Lee. You want me to be perfect. I'm not. Far from it.

LEE. I don't know what you want us to say. I do my best. Thank you for being in court.

DOMINIC. Did you do some burglaries, Lee?

LEE. Yes.

DOMINIC. What for?

LEE. For money to buy heroin when our kid doesn't give us any.

DOMINIC. Do you take drugs, Lee?

LEE. Yes.

DOMINIC. I don't like people who lie.

LEE. No.

DOMINIC. I didn't know.

LEE. No.

DOMINIC. Why?

LEE. I didn't want to hurt you, Dom.

DOMINIC. I think I can make my mind up about that.

LEE. You can't.

DOMINIC. I can. You should stop.

LEE. I know. It's easier said than done.

DOMINIC. If you don't I'm not going to speak to you.

LEE. I've tried, you idiot.

DOMINIC. I'm not an idiot. It's not good enough in my opinion. You musn't have tried as hard as you should. You're lucky.

LEE. Yeh, I know.

DOMINIC. I'm glad you know because it's true. It's harder for me. There are many things I would like to do.

DOMINIC *thinks.*

I'm being your friend.

KERRY *goes to* DOMINIC.

KERRY. Well done.

FREYA. Yes.

DOMINIC *snatches the Gameboy off his mother. He sits with his knees up and plays with it.*

DOMINIC. I will be your friend. I was only joking.

LEE. You don't know when you're ahead, Dom.

DOMINIC. Why do you want to protect me, Lee? I'm sick and tired of it. It goes for all of you. Including you, Kerry. How am I ever going to live on my own? I wish someone would tell me why my dad is my granddad. It's not much to ask.

KERRY *wanders away to the table.*

Where's she going, Mum?

FREYA. To get some lemonade. Aren't you, Kerry?

KERRY. Yes.

KERRY *pours some lemonade into her glass.*

I don't care, you know. I think it's brilliant. It's unique. I suppose yer going to tell us it's not true. It always happens to us. I've never felt this special before. Is he your father, Freya?

FREYA. Yes.

KERRY. Is he your son?

JOACHIM. Where are you?

KERRY. I'm here.

JOACHIM. Of course he is my son.

KERRY. Dom.

> DOMINIC *looks up from playing the Gameboy.*

DOMINIC. What?

KERRY. Did you hear?

DOMINIC. Yes. I'm busy.

FREYA. Dominic.

DOMINIC. What?

FREYA. Put it away.

> DOMINIC *makes a grumbling noise and puts the Gameboy in his pocket.*

DOMINIC. It was nearly my best ever score. What is it? It had better be important.

> FREYA *runs her fingers through* DOMINIC*'s hair.*

FREYA. It's nothing.

DOMINIC. It must be something, Mum.

FREYA. You didn't listen to Kerry.

DOMINIC. I did. My dad is my granddad. I know that. I want to know why? I've given up waiting.

FREYA. I have told you.

DOMINIC. Yes. It's hard to take it in though.

FREYA. I know. Your father is also my father.

DOMINIC. Ah. I didn't know that. Is he?

FREYA. Yes.

DOMINIC. It's funny. Why?

FREYA. Well, what do people do when they're in love with each other?

DOMINIC. I'm not getting this, Mum. It's hard to think the right thoughts. Can we just talk about me getting a flat? There's someone at work. He wants to get a flat and share it with me. We've worked out the finance.

FREYA. You are not sharing a flat with someone we don't know.

DOMINIC. I am.

FREYA. You're not.

DOMINIC. With Lee then. Me and Lee could get a flat together.

LEE. We couldn't, Dom.

DOMINIC. Why?

LEE. We just couldn't.

DOMINIC. That's not an answer.

LEE. You deserve better.

DOMINIC. I don't. I don't want any better.

LEE. I'm more trouble than I'm worth. Fuck off. I'm fuckin' sick of yer.

*LEE goes out. KERRY starts to go after him.*

FREYA. Leave him.

KERRY. You know what he'll be doing.

FREYA. Yes.

KERRY. He only did it for an excuse.

*LEE enters. He goes to the table and pours some lemonade into his glass.*

JOACHIM. Is that Kerry?

LEE. It's me.

JOACHIM. Where is she?

KERRY. I'm here.

*JOACHIM puts the bucket on the floor.*

JOACHIM. Come. Come. Come.

*KERRY goes to him. JOACHIM finds a bentwood chair which he brings back to the table.*

Sit.

*KERRY sits on the chair. JOACHIM wipes his hands on the damp cloth. He sits on the stool. He begins to feel around her face with the palms of his hands. He applies a lot of pressure. KERRY tries to pull away.*

KERRY. You're hurting us.

JOACHIM. Be still.

   KERRY *is still.*

KERRY. Yer hands are mucky for a kick off.

JOACHIM. Next time, you will not wear lipstick.

KERRY. I'll do what I want. There won't be a next time.

JOACHIM. You will do as I demand.

KERRY. Keep yer hair on.

   JOACHIM *runs his hands through the full length of her hair.*

JOACHIM. My hands are dirty. You will need to wash your hair after every session.

   JOACHIM *tears away at the clay on the armature, smoothing bits over and pulling other bits off to put them elsewhere.*

   I want to do the full figure, but I always start with the head.

KERRY. Are you going to put this in a book or something?

JOACHIM. Maybe someone will. Who can tell?

KERRY. Will I be famous?

JOACHIM. No. I will be famous because of you.

   JOACHIM *wipes his hands on the cloth. He begins to feel around* KERRY*'s face.*

   LEE *goes to* DOMINIC.

DOMINIC. Very nice, I musn't say.

LEE. Budge up.

   LEE *perches on the chair.* FREYA *kneels.*

FREYA. Would you think about sharing a flat?

LEE. No. It's the way it is, Dom. I can't be trusted.

DOMINIC. That's just where you're wrong. You can change and grow-up. I have to say this. It's because I'll always be stuck. I don't want to be. That's the way it is, Lee. You're way is just rubbish. And if you cared about me, you'd say yes, you would share a flat. I'm going to play on the computer.

DOMINIC *gets up and goes out.*

LEE. Phew. Has she been talking to him?

FREYA. Mmm, I think so.

LEE. It's amazing. You heard the duty solicitor. He said two
years if I was lucky.

FREYA. We would find the money.

LEE. For ever?

FREYA. Yes, it would be forever. It's a lot to ask someone who
doesn't think he's any good.

LEE. It fuckin' is. He'll be wondering where I am.

LEE *gets up and goes out.*

JOACHIM *takes a knife, spoon and fork from his jacket
pocket. He begins to model the clay with the end of the
knife.* FREYA *goes to the table.*

FREYA. Well done you.

KERRY. Why, what have I done?

FREYA. You've stirred him up a bit.

KERRY. Is that good?

FREYA. Yes.

KERRY. It's fortunate. I've gone off him. He's useless. He
doesn't know what day it is half the week.

*A slight pause.*

What?

*A slight pause.*

I don't mean half what I say yer know.

JOACHIM. She tests everyone.

JOACHIM *spits on the knife.*

To see how much people like her.

JOACHIM *is working slowly, minutely.*

I do believe you are not interested in conditional love. It has
to be everything or nothing. But then again, I do not care
one jot for psychoanalysis. I am more feudal. It is an

excuse, not a good one I might add, for punishment and repression, and for passing the blame on. It is not any kind of enlightenment.

JOACHIM *puts the knife in the breast pocket of his jacket. He feels* KERRY*'s face with the ends of his fingers, particularly her lips and nose.*

KERRY. It doesn't look like us much.

JOACHIM. Patience is required. Keep your mouth still which I know you find hard to do.

KERRY. It tickles.

JOACHIM. Yes, I am always right.

KERRY. Has he done you, Freya?

JOACHIM. Of course.

KERRY. Yer nowt but a bully. I asked her. Was Dominic a mistake?

FREYA. If he was I'm glad. Don't you think he is?

KERRY. Yeh.

JOACHIM *takes the knife. He works on the clay around the nose and the mouth.*

Have you other children and that?

KERRY *leans forward and touches* JOACHIM.

I was asking you.

JOACHIM. Yes, I believe so. I've six or so children. Have I, Freya?

FREYA. You know how many, Joachim. Dominic is the seventh. Of the others, I was the youngest.

KERRY. It gets to us.

FREYA. What?

KERRY. That yer like us sort of thing. It's a story, I know that much. I've not had a story of me own before. I'm chuffed to death. I won't tell any one.

DOMINIC *enters followed by* LEE.

DOMINIC. Mum, where are those coloured lights?

FREYA. What d'you want them for?

DOMINIC. We're going to put them up in the garden.

FREYA. They're in the attic.

LEE *and* DOMINIC *go out.*

KERRY. How did it happen – you know?

FREYA. Like this. Joachim was doing my face.

KERRY. Yer not guilty or anything.

FREYA. Should I be? Would it help you if I was?

KERRY. No. I'm guilty about stuff I've done wrong. Me mam would go bananas if she knew. She thinks everyone should be punished. She does. It's only because everyone punishes her, I suppose. I've not thought about it. You know what she does.

KERRY *leans forward and touches* JOACHIM *who stops for a moment.*

She chucks stuff at prison vans. You'd hate her.

JOACHIM *works on the clay.*

You know your other children.

KERRY *touches* JOACHIM.

JOACHIM. Yes.

KERRY. Where do they live?

JOACHIM. In Denmark, in Czechoslovakia, in Germany, in Holland, in Paris where I lived for a long time with Freya's mother before she died.

KERRY. Were you blind when you were born?

JOACHIM. If I was to tell you I had never seen a colour, what would you say?

KERRY. I don't know. I'd say you was. Oh.

JOACHIM *puts the knife in his jacket pocket.*

Is it ever going to look like us?

JOACHIM. I do not expect it to, to your satisfaction, but to mine I hope so.

JOACHIM *takes some wooden and wire-ended modelling
tools from the inside pocket of his jacket. He takes off the
rubber band that is holding them together.*

KERRY. I never know if I believe you.

JOACHIM *feels her ears and her cheeks.*

JOACHIM. You make demons of people like everyone of your
class.

KERRY. I beg your pardon?

JOACHIM. Am I the devil that makes you feel holy? Is that
why you wish to know all about me?

FREYA. Joachim.

JOACHIM. Be quiet. Making demons of people is a sign of
moral bankruptcy.

KERRY. Oh. I was at the back of the queue when brains was
handed out.

JOACHIM *smiles.*

JOACHIM. You have a little cyst.

KERRY. I've always had it.

JOACHIM. Like your cleverness. You are the same as me and
always get everything you want. Where are you, Freya?

FREYA. Here.

JOACHIM. She gets nothing she needs. She is too
understanding. You are different.

FREYA. Don't be silly.

JOACHIM. Be quiet. She was the youngest. I had to keep one
of them. You should take Lee because she won't.

FREYA. Joachim.

JOACHIM. My other children are fools, too. Life can be good,
but they do not know it. They are reluctant and cowardly,
unlike you and me.

JOACHIM *searches through the tools. He finds one with a
flat wooden end and uses it to work on the clay.*

Even as a young boy I was fascinated by the smell of a
woman. I have loved quite a few in order to prove to myself

that I could not live on my own. She is itching to apologise for me. In Denmark we are taught from a young age not to think too highly of ourselves. She should live there. I went away because of that to Germany, then to Amsterdam, where I made my name modelling the whores around the Geldersekade. My mother was ordinary. She was a cook in a bottle factory, and it was a struggle for her to bring me up on her own. She was quite fierce. In Europe I was stateless, with not a care in the world. Freya was born in Paris, though her mother was English. When she died, her grandparents took her from me. I was merely the money that brought her up. We met again when she was twenty seven and I was already an old man. Sixty nine or thereabouts. It was she who insisted we look for a quiet place to live, for our child, for Dominic. Lee has made it a little noisier since the day he stole her apples, and she rewarded him with a glass of lemonade.

KERRY. Have you ever done him?

JOACHIM. Of course. Lee has been round the world, aged twelve. Two boys naked together. He and my son. You will be pleased to know it is very, very famous.

KERRY. Oh. Is it rude or something?

JOACHIM. No, it is innocent.

KERRY. He's hardly that.

JOACHIM. You get succour from the demons that are in people.

KERRY. I haven't a clue what yer on about.

JOACHIM *puts the tool in his breast pocket.*

JOACHIM. What a weakness that is.

KERRY. Yer talking about yerself, aren't yer.

JOACHIM. Yes.

KERRY. Oh.

FREYA. Joachim.

JOACHIM. Do not interrupt me.

KERRY. You're just rude.

JOACHIM. Yes.

KERRY. Don't apologise in a hurry, I wouldn't.

JOACHIM. Yes, I know. Where are your hands.

> JOACHIM *takes hold of* KERRY's *hands and feels her fingers.*

> It is going to take me a few months to get anything good at all. You can live here. There are some sessions when I will want you to be silent, others when I will expect you to talk. I will begin in here, for the preliminary work, before we move to my studio. I warn you now, it is very slow and you will become restless. Please. Come prepared to think. I want to hear you, even on the days when we are quiet.

KERRY. Hang on. I know you. What do I get out of it?

JOACHIM. Perhaps very little, as happened with Lee. Perhaps something special. I can promise you nothing. It is up to you, and it is up to me. If it does not work out then we will stop, and you will not go round the world. I believe you want it to continue.

KERRY. Yeh, I do.

JOACHIM. Then it will.

KERRY. Is this more of the rules you were on about?

JOACHIM. Some of them.

KERRY. They're not rules, far as I can tell.

JOACHIM. You agree to go ahead?

KERRY. Yeh, I do. Thanks.


## Scene Four

*The garden. Early the following morning.*

*The apple tree is full of coloured lights. The bulbs are lit and shine out into the pale, watery sunlight.*

EWAN *comes on followed by* HAZEL. HAZEL *has a carrier bag full of rags.*

*The church clock a few hundred yards away begins to chime six o'clock.*

EWAN *puts the iron key on the nail on the tree.* HAZEL *puts her hands on her knees and tries to breath. They talk quietly.*

EWAN. It was me climbed over. What's wrong with yer? You was like Boadicea.

HAZEL. I've got one of me asthma attacks.

*She holds out the carrier bag.*

It's this bloody stink of petrol.

KERRY *enters from the house.*

KERRY. Oh Jesus.

EWAN. Now then. Kerry, Kerry.

KERRY. What the hell are you doing, as if I couldn't guess.

HAZEL *takes an inhaler from her pocket and uses it.*

EWAN. Yer making yer mam poorly. Can't yer see?

KERRY. Go fuck yerself, Ewan.

EWAN. I might do that, except I'll fuck you first.

KERRY *sniffs.*

KERRY. Something reeks more than you.

*She goes to her mother to the carrier bag. She pulls out the end of a shirt.* EWAN *takes a box of matches from his pocket and lights one. He lets it fall.*

Yer know what you are? Yer nowt but hysterical.

KERRY *throws the carrier bag away.*

HAZEL. He's more pervy than a pervert.

KERRY. You've got him wrong, Mam.

HAZEL. He'll have you at it if yer not careful.

EWAN *goes to the wall. He searches for a loose brick.*

KERRY. Yer taken up with him?

HAZEL. Yeh. Anything against it?

KERRY. Yer don't like him, Mam.

HAZEL. It's up to me who I like. He don't do no harm.

EWAN *has found a brick. He begins to scrape away the loose concrete to get it out.*

EWAN. I thought you'd be asleep. Kerry, Kerry. Tucked up and snug.

KERRY. Yer mad.

EWAN *has the brick. He throws it into the air and catches it.*

EWAN. Smash a few windows. Put a few flames through the letter box.

KERRY. Lee's in there.

EWAN. He fucked yer yet?

KERRY. No.

EWAN. He's a heroin addict, yer dozy fuckin' ponce. Hard-on gets a bigger hard-on. He's fuckin' not capable of a wank. He's fuckin' impotent. Hasn't he told yer?

KERRY. He might have done.

EWAN. My backside he has. Yer a naïve lass.

KERRY. I was going for a walk.

EWAN. He'll be nice and limp when he sleeps with yer. Kerry, Kerry.

KERRY. He has his own room. We all do.

EWAN. It's a bit chaste for me.

KERRY. Yeh, it is. It's how I like it from now on.

JOACHIM *enters from the house. He is wearing white trousers and a white shirt which is not tucked in. He has bare feet.* KERRY *goes to him.*

It's not me I promise yer. I'll give yer anything.

JOACHIM *puts his arm around her.*

JOACHIM. I know. Is it Ewan?

EWAN. Yeh. It's a bit much is that, coming from you.

JOACHIM. You people, all you do is destroy what is good.

EWAN. That's even better like.

JOACHIM. Where are you? With Lee you were welcome once upon a time, against my judgement.

JOACHIM *is trying to find him.*

EWAN. I'm here.

EWAN *moves.*

JOACHIM. You hurt someone and you do not care twopence.
You people, you take a life and I believe you care even less.

EWAN. Over here.

HAZEL. What's he on about, Ewan?

EWAN. You more than likely, isn't he?

HAZEL. I don't know.

HAZEL *uses the inhaler.*

EWAN. Oy.

JOACHIM. I met your type a hundred times in the back streets
of Naples.

EWAN *moves.*

EWAN. Really?

JOACHIM. Oh, I think so. All the flotsam and jetsam of the
low-life. As with every pimp in the world, you have a
complete disregard for a woman.

HAZEL. He's on about something.

EWAN. You'd wish yer didn't know. Take it from me.

KERRY. Yer warped, Ewan. You'd set the house on fire with
yer brother in it.

EWAN. Would I hell. I was going along with her.

KERRY. What about us, Mam?

HAZEL. Like he said. I was going along with him. Did you do
Dennis in or something?

EWAN. Like hell I did. I've no fuckin' reason to.

FREYA *enters. She is wearing a nightdress and the
bathrobe. She has bare feet.*

You don't scare us. None of yus do.

EWAN *moves.*

Over here yer dozy pillock.

DOMINIC *enters. His hair is ruffled. He is wearing jeans
and a tee shirt. He has bare feet.*

How yer doing, Hard-on?

DOMINIC *yawns.*

DOMINIC. What's going on, Mum?

FREYA. I'm not sure.

HAZEL. Let's go. I can't breathe any road up.

EWAN *threatens* JOACHIM *with the brick.*

EWAN. It'll be a pleasure to use it on yer.

JOACHIM *locates him.* EWAN *moves.*

I'll have yer dancing like a bear.

JOACHIM. What do you want?

EWAN. It's a bit of a liberty, I reckon.

JOACHIM. What is?

EWAN. The way you pick and choose. And her. And yer precious Freya. I adored her once. Don't panic. Only in the way that children love and adore. I don't want to make too much of it, Freya, but you picked Lee. I'm the soft one. I was the big softy. Still are. I was the oldest brother. There isn't much more to it than that.

LEE *enters. He is wearing jeans. He has bare feet.*

Now then, our kid. How's it going?

LEE. Yeh. Now then, our lad. What yer doing?

EWAN. I'm off, kid.

LEE. What've yer come for like?

EWAN. You'll never know.

EWAN *takes two tin foil sachets from his pocket.*

LEE. Thanks.

DOMINIC. Is that some drugs, Lee?

LEE. Yeh.

EWAN. Yer been in court, our lad.

LEE. Yeh.

EWAN. Me mam said.

EWAN *goes to wall. He puts the sachets in the hole and replaces the brick.*

KERRY. Yer must want him like he is to make you feel good, I wouldn't be surprised.

EWAN. I won't see yus.

HAZEL. You off? Where yer going?

EWAN. Nowhere for you.

EWAN *starts to go.* FREYA *goes towards him.*

FREYA. Wait.

EWAN. I fuckin' killed someone, yer dozy twat. She would have had us fuckin' kill you.

EWAN *goes.*

HAZEL. He's twisted. I was right the first time.

KERRY. I don't believe you, Mam.

HAZEL. Only kidding yer.

HAZEL *uses the inhaler.*

KERRY. Where d'you get the petrol?

HAZEL. Where d'you get petrol?

KERRY. A garage.

HAZEL. Yer know then, don't yer. Only a joke. You have everything. You couldn't be more luckier. D'you think we'd do it?

KERRY. Yeh.

HAZEL. I'd do more than that, no problem.

FREYA *goes towards her.*

Get off. Who needs you.

FREYA *stops.* HAZEL *takes a packet of cigarettes from her pocket.*

You're a piece of filth an' all. Oy.

JOACHIM. Who? Me?

HAZEL. Who else is the filth round here?

HAZEL *lights a cigarette.*

I'm going. Don't worry. Once I've had my say.

*She smokes. Her hand is shaking.*

All right, I've had my say.

HAZEL *starts to go.* FREYA *goes after her.* HAZEL *points the cigarette.*

I'll stick this in your eye, no trouble.

FREYA *knocks it out of her hand.*

*A slight pause.*

HAZEL *picks it up. She smokes.*

Yeh. It's two doors along. Lee knows where I am. When yer get sick of her.

HAZEL *goes.*

*There is a short silence.*

JOACHIM. What happened?

FREYA. Everything and nothing, Joachim.

JOACHIM. Has she gone?

FREYA. Yes.

FREYA *goes to the wall. She takes out the heroin. She goes to* LEE. *She holds the sachets in her palm.*

Well?

JOACHIM. What's happening?

FREYA. Be quiet, my love.

JOACHIM. Someone tell me.

FREYA. Later. I'm waiting.

LEE *thinks.*

LEE. It's not my fault.

FREYA. I don't care whose fault it is. It's up to you.

LEE. What are the options like?

FREYA. You tell me.

LEE. I asked you.

FREYA. None as far as I'm concerned.

JOACHIM. Freya –

FREYA. I'm busy with someone else.

LEE *thinks.*

LEE. I won't do it.

FREYA. Won't you.

KERRY. Listen to her. Please. She knows like you said. She knows all sorts. She knows what it's like.

JOACHIM *goes towards the house.*

DOMINIC. Where're you going, Dad?

FREYA. I won't be long, Joachim.

JOACHIM *raises his hand to acknowledge her. He goes.*

DOMINIC. Is he melancholy, Mum?

FREYA. I expect so.

DOMINIC. Does that mean we'll have to listen to him be silent all day?

FREYA *smiles.*

FREYA. Not unless you want to.

DOMINIC. Can I watch him do Kerry?

FREYA. Yes.

DOMINIC. He might get angry.

FREYA *whispers in* DOMINIC*'s ear.*

FREYA. If you were very quiet, he wouldn't know. You choose. I'm making no more decisions.

*She looks at* LEE.

Well?

LEE *is silent.* FREYA *screws up the sachets. She goes to the carrier bag. She looks inside, gingerly.*

An old shirt. It looks like some pyjamas. Several socks.

KERRY. Yeh. I'll get rid of it.

FREYA. It doesn't bare thinking about, Lee, does it?

LEE. Why me? What is it?

KERRY. Can't yer stink it?

LEE. Yeh.

FREYA. He's your brother for goodness sake.

LEE. She's her mother. So what?

FREYA. Well, it's up to you from now on. And up to you, Kerry.

FREYA *goes to* KERRY.

Well done.

KERRY. What for?

FREYA. You'll see.

FREYA *goes.*

KERRY. What does she mean?

LEE. How should I know.

KERRY. I can't wait. You know her better than us.

LEE. I don't.

KERRY. She loves you.

LEE. She doesn't.

KERRY. She does. Doesn't she, Dominic?

DOMINIC. You've always been her favourite person out of everybody.

LEE. I haven't.

DOMINIC. Yes.

LEE. Yeh, I know.

DOMINIC *goes to the carrier bag.*

KERRY. Leave it, Dominic.

DOMINIC *stops. He looks at the sky.*

I don't think she realised, not properly. He didn't, I know that much. They live in their own world a bit, don't they.

LEE. Yeh. What is it then?

KERRY. They were going to set the house on fire with us lot in it. You're sleep walking, you are. You want to wake up a bit and let it through.

DOMINIC. You know something, Kerry. It's clouding over.

LEE. Yeh.

KERRY. Yeh what?

LEE. Just yeh. They're torture units.

KERRY. What?

LEE. Prisons. I can't do it again.

KERRY. Have you had a toot this morning?

LEE. No. I haven't got any. She's got it. I won't stop. It's the way it is. Yer have to see things as they are.

KERRY. I'm not going to. I don't want to, I refuse.

LEE. I am.

KERRY. You'll die then.

LEE. So I'm going to die. It makes no difference.

KERRY. It does to me.

LEE. Freya's gone off us.

KERRY. Why don't yer feel sorry for yourself, I would if I was pathetic.

KERRY *goes to* DOMINIC. *She talks in his ear.*

Go and tell him you don't like him.

DOMINIC *goes to* LEE.

DOMINIC. I like you, Lee.

LEE *smiles.*

KERRY. Dominic.

DOMINIC *goes to* KERRY.

Go and ask him if he's going to feel sorry for himself all his life.

DOMINIC *goes to* LEE.

DOMINIC. Are you going to feel sorry for yourself all your life?

LEE. Course not.

DOMINIC. If you die, I'll be extremely angry.

DOMINIC *talks in* LEE*'s ear.*

Go and ask her why you're going to die.

LEE *goes to* KERRY.

LEE. He wants to know why I'm going to die.

KERRY. Go and tell him you're not because I won't let you.

LEE *goes to* DOMINIC.

LEE. She says she won't let me.

DOMINIC. I won't either.

KERRY. Dominic.

DOMINIC *goes to* KERRY.

Go and tell him I love him.

DOMINIC. No. I won't. I'll tell him anything else.

KERRY. Please.

DOMINIC. No. Why should I?

*A slight pause.*

KERRY. I don't see why you should.

*She runs her hand down* DOMINIC*'s arm.*

Sorry.

DOMINIC. I like him so I understand it.

KERRY *goes to* LEE.

KERRY. If you ever hurt him, I'll fucking kill you. You listening to me. It's a real fucking promise. So what yer going to do?

LEE. Yeh.

KERRY. Yeh what? Yeh, yeh, yeh, yeh, yeh.

LEE. Yes, I'll try. I haven't any. I don't have a choice.

KERRY. He doesn't have a choice Monday, Tuesday, Wednesday, Thursday, Friday, Saturday, Sunday, Monday, Tuesday, Wednesday, Thursday, Friday, Saturday, Sunday. Which day are you going to choose?

LEE. I suppose I'll have to choose today.

KERRY. You suppose?

LEE. Yes.

*DOMINIC goes to them.*

DOMINIC. What's going on?

KERRY. I'm trying to get him to promise a few things.

*DOMINIC whispers in KERRY's ear.*

He says I have to tell you he's jealous.

DOMINIC. I didn't say that.

LEE. What did you say?

DOMINIC. It's for me to know and you to find out.

*DOMINIC goes.*

KERRY. He said he loved me, which is more than you do.

*A slight pause.*

LEE. I don't want to let you down. I only would.

KERRY. I know that one. I've used it myself.

LEE. It's true.

KERRY. It was true when I used it an' all, sort of.

*KERRY walks away.*

*Silence.*

I'm shy, believe it or not. Shy of you any road up.

LEE. Why?

KERRY. I'm frightened.

*A slight pause.*

LEE. Are you?

KERRY. Yeh.

LEE. I am.

*A slight pause.*

I'm not much good.

KERRY. You should let other people decide.

*A slight pause.*

You know your trouble, you don't want to believe it.

LEE. What?

*A slight pause.*

KERRY. I don't know really.

LEE *goes towards her.*

Go away. I don't want yer.

LEE *stops.*

You'd only be pretending, wouldn't yer?

LEE. I can't say. No. Will yer be with us? If things are possible for you, does that mean it's possible for me?

KERRY. Yes.

LEE. I see it is for you. I did a few days ago. I do. Yeh.

*He takes a step or two towards her.*

That's the thing about heroin and me, we never know owt. I'm never sure.

KERRY. You were jealous of Ewan.

LEE. Yeh, I was.

KERRY. What's happened since?

LEE. Someone's dead.

KERRY. Yes.

*The lights on the apple tree go out.*

LEE. Guess who.

KERRY. Yes.

*The End.*